For

Article 9 of the U.C.C.

Secured Transactions

With Selected Bankruptcy Statutes

And Other U.C.C. Provisions

BY:

Jack S. Ezon, Esq.

and

Jeffrey S. Dweck, Esq.

Law Rules Publishing Corporation
Old Tappan, NJ 07675

1997

(800) 371-1271

Third Edition

Library of Congress Catalog Card Number: 95-75005
ISBN #: 1-887-42624-8

LAW RULES PUBLISHING CORPORATION
River Vale, New Jersey

NOTE: E-Z Rules is not a substitute for the actual text of the Uniform Commercial Code and should not be quoted or cited to. E-Z Rules is meant to be used as a quick reference and guide to understanding Article 9 of the Uniform Commercial Code, and cannot completely replace it. In addition, the "overview" for each section of the "Roadmap to Article 9" is not meant to be a comprehensive teaching tool. It is merely meant to remind the reader of certain key points.

To my mentor,
David Haddad
and to
Jack Haddad
for your constant
support, advice,
and for always being
there.

<u>USING E-Z RULES FOR SECURED TRANSACTIONS</u>

Welcome to E-Z Rules, a new way of presenting rules and laws, designed to put the "ease" into *legalese*!

E-Z Rules translates the confusing statutory language of the UCC into plain and simple English. E-Z Rules are designed to give you quick access to important information you often need, without the unnecessary strain of dissecting long, monotonous, statutory texts. And remember, E-Z Rules does this WITHOUT EXCLUDING ANY KEY POINTS OF THE ACTUAL RULE OR STATUTE!

E-Z Rules is easy to use. It has been carefully tailored to meet the needs of both the law student and today's active law firm. In order to take full advantage of the E-Z Rules system, it would be beneficial to review some of its features:

* The rules are **boldly** titled for quick spotting.

* E-Z Rules is laid out so that the entire substance of a rule or statute could be grasped at a single glance.

* All rules follow the format of the Uniform Commercial Code. Where the actual subsection of the rule is used, it is enclosed between parenthesis "( )." <u>All other numbers and letters are produced by E-Z Rules</u> and therefore, should not be cited to when discussing a rule. "E-Z Rules bullets" have been added in addition to the official sub-sections found in the actual code in order to make the substance more comprehensive.

For Example, in §9-318 there are four sections, referred to in E-Z Rules as (1) - (4). These are actual sections used in the U.C.C. and may be called, for example, "subsection (1)." Under subsection (1) there are two subsections, (a) - (b).

Since these are surrounded by parentheses, these, too, may be referenced by their names (ex: "§9-318(1)(a)"). Under §9-318(2), however, there are items labeled "a.", "1.", and so forth. Since these are not enclosed in parenthesis, they are not the letters used by the Uniform Commercial Code.

* Key words and phrases are emphasized with either **bold**, *italic*, or <u>underline</u>. Some words begin with Capital Letters in order to emphasize them. This not only helps in making the rules easier to understand, but has been proven to help the user focus in on pivotal words or phrases, which may otherwise go unnoticed. In addition, certain words have been abbreviated in order to facilitate quick referencing and easier reading.

Note: E-Z Rules are not a substitute for the actual text of the UCC, and should not be quoted or cited to. E-Z Rules is meant to be used as a quick reference and guide to understanding Article 9 of the UCC, and cannot completely replace it. In addition, the "overview" for each section of the "Roadmap to Article 9" is not meant to be a comprehensive teaching tool. It is merely meant to remind the reader of certain key points.

Since these are surrounded by parentheses, these, too, may be referenced by their names (ex: "§9-318(1)(a)"). Under §9-318(2), however, there are items labeled "a.", "1.", and so forth. Since these are not enclosed in parenthesis, they are not the letters used by the Uniform Commercial Code.

* Key words and phrases are emphasized with either **bold**, *italic*, or <u>underline</u>. Some words begin with Capital Letters in order to emphasize them. This not only helps in making the rules easier to understand, but has been proven to help the user focus in on pivotal words or phrases, which may otherwise go unnoticed. In addition, certain words have been abbreviated in order to facilitate quick referencing and easier reading.

Note: E-Z Rules are not a substitute for the actual text of the UCC, and should not be quoted or cited to. E-Z Rules is meant to be used as a quick reference and guide to understanding Article 9 of the UCC, and cannot completely replace it. In addition, the "overview" for each section of the "Roadmap to Article 9" is not meant to be a comprehensive teaching tool. It is merely meant to remind the reader of certain key points.

Supplement to:

E-Z RULES®

For

Article 9 of the U.C.C.

Secured Transactions

Reflecting Changes for

The Revised Proposed Article 9

BY:

Jack S. Ezon, Esq.

and

Jeffrey S. Dweck, Esq.

LAW RULES PUBLISHING CORPORATION
River Vale, New Jersey
2000

(800) 371-1321

1-201(19) Revised Article 9 requires the "*observance of reasonable commercial standards of fair dealing*" in addition to "honesty in fact" (R: 9-102(a)(43)).

9-102(1)(b) The Scope of Revised Article 9 is expanded cover the following additional items:

a. Sale of Payment Intangibles – (R: 9-102(a)(61) and 9-109(a)(3)).

b. Sale of Promissory Notes – which are Instruments that are not "order" paper (like checks) or CDs (R: 9-102(a)(65) and 9-109(a)(3)).

c. "Hybrid" Chattel Paper – Chattel Paper covering unidentifiable Goods can be secured *to the extent* it is sold with specified Goods. For example, obligations secured by software are covered by Article 9, but only *to the extent* that the software is sold in an integrated transaction with specific Goods (such as a computer) (R: 9-102(a)(11)).

d. Electronic Chattel Paper - Chattel Paper need not be in writing to be included in Revised Article 9 as long as it is "stored in an electronic medium" instead of in tangible form (R: 9-102(a)(31) and 9-330).

e. Insurance Claims – Revised Article 9 will permit S/Is in health-care receivables held by health-care providers as *original* collateral (and not just proceeds) (R: 9-102(a)(46) and 9-109(d)(8)).

f. Consignments – Article 9 will apply to all consignment transactions (which will be treated like PMSIs) excluding consignments of consumer goods and consignments of "small transactions" (R: 9-102(a)(20); 9-102(a)(21); 9-109(a)(4)).

g. Notes Secured by Real Estate – Article 9 will apply to a S/I in a mortgage note (though not the mortgage itself) (R: 9-109(b) and 9-203(g)).

h. Deposit Accounts – *except in consumer transactions.* This would include an ordinary bank account (R: 9-109).

i. Letter-of-Credit Rights – though Revised Article 9 does not cover a right to draw under a letter of credit (9-102(a)(51); 9-109(c)(4); 9-203(f)(2)).

j. Tort Claims – "commercial tort claims" arising out of the borrower's business or profession will be covered by Revised Article 9 as long as they do not arise out of after-acquired property or personal injury (R: 9-102(a)(13); 9-109(d)(12); 9-204(b)(2)).

k. Agricultural Liens – which are non-possessory or statutory (R: 9-109).

l. Investment Property – as defined in Article 8 (R: 9-102(a)(49); 9-106; 9-312(a); 9-314).

m. Software – only if the Software is "embedded" in goods and becomes a *part of* the goods will it constitute goods (R: 9-102)(a)(44); 9-102(a)(75); 9-103).

n. Supporting Obligations – including a guaranty of payment or a letter of credit supporting an obligation to pay money (R: 9-102(a)(77); 9-203(f)).

9-103 Revised Article 9 : All filing will be done in the state where the Debtor was formed (R: 9-301(1)). Filing for foreign debtors in a jurisdiction without a public filing system would be done in Washington D.C. (R: 9-307(e)). Otherwise, the law governing perfection will depend on the type of collateral secured:

- *Perfection by Possession*, the law of the state of where the collateral is located will govern perfection (R: 9-301(2)).
- *Fixture Filings*, the law of the jurisdiction in which the fixtures are located will govern perfection (R: 9-301(3)(A)).
- *Goods covered by a Certificate of Title* - The law of the jurisdiction under whose certificate of title the goods are covered will govern perfection (R: 9-303).
- *Letter of Credit Rights* – The local law of the issuer's jurisdiction (or a nominated person's) will govern perfection, unless a S/I is perfected only under Revised 9-308(d) (Perfection of a S/I in a supporting obligation for collateral by perfecting a S/I in the collateral itself) (R: 9-306).
- *Deposit Accounts* – The local law of a bank's jurisdiction will govern perfection (R: 9-304).

- *Investment Property* –
  - *Certificated Securities* – the law of the jurisdiction where the certificate is located (R:9-305(a)(1)).
  - *Uncertificated Securities* – the law of the jurisdiction where the Issuer is located (R:9-305(a)(2)).
  - *Entitlements/Securities Accounts*– the law of the jurisdiction where the Securities Intermediary is located (R:9-305(a)(3)).
- *Commodity Contract/ Commodity Accounts*– the law of the jurisdiction where the Commodity Intermediary is located (R:9-305(a)(4)).

9-103(d) Revised Article 9 : extends the four-month rule to S/I's perfected by a means other than filing and extends it to <u>1 year</u> after the Debtor moves into a new jurisdiction when collateral is:

1. Transferred to a new debtor

and 2. The new Debtor moves to another jurisdiction

9-104(l) Revised Article 9 : Deposit Accounts will be included within the scope of Revised Article 9 as long as they are not deposit accounts securing a consumer transaction. Deposit Accounts may only be perfected by "control" (R: 9-102(a)(29); 9-104; 9-312(b); 9-314).

9-105(1)(c) Revised Article 9 will expand the definition of "Collateral" to explicitly include (1) proceeds subject to a S/I, (2) property subject to an agricultural lien and (3) payment intangibles and promissory notes that have not been sold (R: 9-102(a)(12)).

9-106 Revised Article 9 : The definition of "Accounts" will be expanded to include any "payment obligations" arising out of the sale, lease or license of many kinds of tangible or intangible property (including credit card receivables, lottery winnings and health-care insurance receivables or receivables for services rendered or to be rendered). This revised definition will cause many General Intangibles to be classified as "Accounts" (excluding money, investment property, letter of credit proceeds, deposit accounts, tort claims or rights to payment evidenced by chattel paper) (9-102(a)(2); 9-109(a)(3)).

9-107 Revised Article 9 extends the definition of PMSI to include consignments (R: 9-103(d)).

9-110 Revised Article 9 : Generic "safe harbor" terms such as "Inventory," "Accounts," and "Investment Property," will be acceptable under Revised Article 9 , although a super-generic phrase such as "all Debtor's property" will not be sufficient. More detail will be required in consumer transactions and for commercial tort claims (R: 9-108).

9-112 Revised Article 9 : Although a Consignee of Goods or Seller (of Accounts, Chattel Paper, Promissory Notes or Payment Intangibles) does not "own" the property, Revised Article 9 will permit the Consignee or Seller to grant a S/I or sell them to another Buyer. This subsequent sale or S/I will be effective *to the extent* that the first Buyer or Consignor has not perfected its S/I (R: 9-203(b)(2); 9-318; 9-319)).

9-115(4)(a) Revised Article 9 : Deposit Accounts and Letter-of-Credit rights will also be perfected by "control" under Revised Article 9 (R: 9-312(a); 9-314(a); 9-312(b)(2); 9-314(b)).

9-203(c) Revised Article 9 : Although a Consignee of goods or Seller (of Accounts, Chattel Paper, Promissory Notes or Payment Intangibles) does not "own" the property, Revised Article 9 will permit the Consignee or Seller to grant a S/I or sell them to another Buyer. This subsequent sale or S/I will be effective *to the extent* that the first Buyer or Consignor has not perfected its S/I (R: 9-203(b)(2); 9-31-8; 9-319)).

9-206(1) Revised Article 9 expands the application of this rule to all account debtors (it is not limited to account debtors that have bought or leased goods, as in the current Article 9) (R: 9-403(b)).

9-206(1) Revised Article 9 replaces the words "statute or decision" with "law other than this Article," to include other means of creating a waiver by an account debtor (R: 9-403(f)).

9-301(2) Revised Article 9 has extended this grace period to 20 days (R: 9-317(e)).

9-302(1) Revised Article 9 affords automatic perfection status to (1) the <u>sale</u> of <u>payment intangibles</u> and <u>promissory notes</u> (R: 9-309(3); 9-309(4)) as well as (2) <u>Support Obligations</u> (such as guaranties and letters of credit), but only if the underlying collateral is perfected (R: 9-

102(a)(77); 9-203(f); 9-308(d)).

9-302(1)(b) Revised Article 9 extends this period to 20 days (R: 9-315) and limits the unperfected status to the date it becomes unperfected (whereas under current Article 9, unperfected status is retroactive to the date the collateral is converted to proceeds) (R: 9-315(c)). Further, if (1) the proceeds are *identifiable* cash proceeds and (2) at the time the collateral was converted into identifiable cash proceeds the original collateral was perfected, the S/I in such proceeds will remain perfected indefinitely, regardless of whether the S/I in the original collateral remains perfected.

9-304(3) Revised Article 9 : Perfection by possession by a third party (such as a Bailee) will only be effective when the third party acknowledges that it holds the collateral for the S/P's benefit (R: 9-313(c)(1)). A lessee of collateral will not be required to make such acknowledgment as long as the collateral is being leased in the ordinary course of the Debtor's business (R: 9-312(c)(2)).

9-305 Revised Article 9 : Governing Law - The law of the state where the collateral is located will govern the perfection of a S/I perfected by possession (R: 9-301(2)).

9-305 Revised Article 9 : Perfection by possession by a third party (such as a Bailee) will only be effective when the third party acknowledges that it holds the collateral for the S/P's benefit (R: 9-313(c)(1)). A lessee of collateral will not be required to make such acknowledgement as long as the collateral is being leased in the ordinary course of the Debtor's business (R: 9-312(c)(2)).

9-306(1) Revised Article 9 : The definition of "Proceeds" is expanded to include collections on and distributions on account of collateral which is a Supporting Obligation (R: 9-102(a)(64)).

9-306(1) Revised Article 9 broadens the current rule to cover "*whatever is collected on or distributed on account of*" Investment Property (that is original collateral)(i.e. both cash and stock dividends) (R: 9-102(a)(64)).

9-306(2) Revised Article 9 : The S/P must *intend* to release its S/I in connection with its authorization of the disposition (R: 9-315(a)(1)).

9-306(2) Revised Article 9 : There is no longer a requirement that the property be "*received*" by the Debtor for the property to qualify as proceeds. It is only necessary that the property be traceable (directly or indirectly) to the original collateral.

9-307(1) Revised Article 9 : A BIOC of Goods does not defeat the rights of a S/P that perfects by possession (R: 9:320(e)).

9-307(2) Revised Article 9 : A BIOC of Goods does not defeat the rights of a S/P that perfects by possession (R: 9:320(e)).

9-308 Revised Article 9 : A person who has possession of an Instrument will take priority over a person who perfects an Instrument by any other method (R: 9-330). A purchaser of an Instrument will take priority over a S/I in an Instrument if the S/P: (a) gives Value, (b) takes the Instrument in good faith and (c) takes the instrument without knowledge that his interest violates the rights of the S/P. This revision will cause a Holder in Due Course to lose priority to a S/P of an Instrument in all cases except when the S/P perfected by filing (R: 9-330; 9-331).

9-308 Revised Article 9 : The holder of a S/I in an Instrument perfected by possession has priority over a S/I perfected by any other method (such as by filing) (R: 9-330(d)).

9-308(a) Revised Article 9 only requires that the purchaser take the Chattel Paper without knowledge that the purchase "violates" the rights of the S/P. Therefore, a purchaser of Chattel Paper who only sees a Financing Statement covering the Chattel Paper will not be deemed to have "knowledge" that purchasing the Chattel Paper would violate the S/P's rights. This is not the case, however, if the Financing Statement or the Chattel Paper specifically indicates that a purchase of the Chattel Paper from the Debtor would violate the rights of the S/P (R: 9-330(a)).

9-312(1) Revised Article 9 includes priority rules relating to Deposit Accounts and Letter-of-Credit rights. (a) A S/P that perfects a S/I in Letter-of-Credit rights by Control prevails over one that perfects by other means (R: 9-329); (b) A Depositary institution's S/I in an account maintained by the Debtor at the Depositary institution will have priority over another S/I unless the S/P (i) obtained a subordination agreement from the depositary institution, or (ii) is named on the account (R: 9-237(3)).

9-312(3) Revised Article 9 extends the priority over Inventory to the extent that it secures purchase money obligations over *other* Inventory (R: 9-103(b)(2)). However, the PMSI directly securing the price of the Inventory (as opposed to those over *other* Inventory ("enabling loans")) will take priority over other PMSIs (R: 9-324(g)).

9-312(3) Revised Article 9 clarifies that this super-priority will include Chattel Paper proceeds if the S/P subsequently purchases the Chattel Paper (i.e. the purchase is deemed for "new value"). This does not extend to "trade-ins" (R: 9-324(b); 9-330(e)).

9-312(4) Revised Article 9 : When there are multiple PMSIs in effect, a PMSI directly securing the price of the collateral (as opposed to those over *other* collateral ("enabling loans")) will take priority over other PMSIs (R: 9-324(g)). Multiple enabling PMSIs will rank in order of filing. For software that is not considered "Goods," a PMSI can exist to the extent the S/P finances the software and the related equipment (where the software is used in an "integrated" transaction (R: 9-103(c))).

9-318(1) Revised Article 9 : An account debtor with a claim against the assignor of an account, chattel paper, or a payment intangible may not obtain an affirmative recovery from the assignee of that obligation. The claim may be asserted against the assignee only to reduce the amount the account debtor owes (R: 9-404(b)).

9-318(3) Revised Article 9 : Notice to pay a S/P is also ineffective (a) to the extent that the assigned agreement (between the account debtor and the seller) limits the account debtor's duty to make payment to a person who is not the seller and (b) if the notice instructs the account debtor to pay the S/P any amount *less than* the full amount due on the assigned agreement (R: 9-406(b)).

9-401(1) Revised Article 9 : All filings, other than fixture filings, shall be filed with the Secretary of State (R: 9-501(a)(2)).

9-402(1) Revised Article 9 : Signatures of the parties are not required (R: 9-502(a)(1)), nor is the address of the S/P. The Debtor need only "authorize" the filing of the Financing Statement (which can be done by signing a security agreement) (R: 9-509).

9-402(1) Revised Article 9 : The F/S may list the name of a party representing the S/P without stating its capacity (R: 9-503(d)).

9-402(1) Revised Article 9 : Generic "safe harbor" terms such as "Inventory," "Accounts," and "Investment Property," will be acceptable under Revised Article 9 , although a super-generic phrase such as "all Debtor's property" will not be sufficient. More detail will be required in consumer transactions and for commercial tort claims (R: 9-108).

9-402(7) Revised Article 9 requires the F/S to state the name of the Debtor as shown on the public records if the Debtor is a "registered organization." If the Debtor is a trust, the F/S must name the official name of the trust, as specified in the "organic documents" and must also specify that the Debtor is a trust (R: 9-503(a)(1)).

9-404(1) Revised Article 9 : A Debtor will be permitted to file a termination statement without the S/P's signature *only* if the S/P failed to send or file a termination statement which it should have. Any other termination statement filing by the Debtor will be ineffective (R: 9-509; 9-513).

9-501(1) Revised Article 9 explicitly states that the default rules apply to secondary obligors on the secured debt as if the secondary obligor were the Debtor (R: 9-601(d)).

9-501(3) Revised Article 9 prohibits the Debtor (and secondary obligor) from waiving the following rights and duties (R: 9-602):

a. Duties relating to the use and operation of Consumer Goods (R: 9-207(b)(4)(c))
b. The duty to collect collateral in a *commercially reasonable* manner (R: 9-607(c))
c. The implicit duty to refrain from a breach of the peace when taking possession

of collateral (R: 9-609)

d. The duty to apply non-cash proceeds of collection in a *commercially reasonable* manner (R: 9-608 and 9-615)

e. The duty to explain the calculation of a surplus or deficiency (R: 9-608(a) and 9-615(d))

f. The right to an accounting concerning collateral (R: 9-210)

g. Rights associated with the disposition of collateral to the S/P, a part related to the S/P or a secondary obligor (R: 9-615(f))

h. The right to limitations on the effectiveness of certain waivers (R: 9-624)

i. The right to hold the S/P liable for failure to comply with Article 9 (R: 9-625)

9-502(1) Revised Article 9 clarifies that a S/P may enforce all clams that the Debtor has against an account debtor (including proceeding against collateral provided to the Debtor by the account debtor) (R: 9-607(a)).

9-504(1) Revised Article 9 : Revised Official Comment 4 indicates that the S/P should engage in a cost-benefit analysis of whether a preparation is appropriate, taking into account the S/P's risk of collecting preparation costs from the proceeds of the collateral or from the Debtor (R: 9:610(a)).

9-504(2) Revised Article 9 : Deficiency Calculation – The following rules have been added:

1. Sale to an Insider: When collateral is sold to an "insider" (S/P, a party related to the S/P, or a guarantor) at a price below what a commercially reasonable sale to a third party would have brought, the deficiency is calculated based on the amount that would have been obtained if sold to a third party (R: 9-615(f)).

2. Noncash Proceeds: The S/P does not have to apply noncash proceeds (e.g. a note from a buyer at a foreclosure sale) to the Debtor's obligation unless it would be *commercially unreasonable* not to do so. If the S/P does apply the noncash proceeds, it must apply them in a *commercially reasonable* manner (R: 9-615(c)).

9-504(3) Revised Article 9 will also require that the S/P provide additional information in consumer goods transactions. Such information will include the description of any liability for a deficiency and the amount the Debtor must pay the S/P for the deficiency (R: 9-616).

9-504(4) Revised Article 9 clarifies that the S/P is deemed to automatically give the warranties relating to title, possession, quiet enjoyment, etc. which normally accompany a *voluntary* disposition of the same kind of property, unless specifically disclaimed (R: 9-610(d)-(f)).

SUMMARY TABLE OF CONTENTS

<u>THE E-Z RULES ROADMAP</u>

One of the most beneficial features of E-Z Rules is its built-in **Roadmap to Article 9.** This section consists of an overview of the key topics of Article 9 and the relevant rules or sections alongside. The "roadmap" places all sections needed for a given topic at your fingertips. Please note that the overview appears in a different typeface than the text of the rule. Also note that where only a portion of a rule is included in the overview, its title is not bolded.

The roadmap will be most beneficial to readers who are looking to analyze problems. By using the roadmap as a checklist, it will help the reader breakdown a problem and "attack" it in a comprehensive and organized fashion and in accordance with the rules.

Studying the Roadmap will also help the reader grasp the concepts behind Article 9 and get an overall picture of the relevant law.

The use of the roadmap is one of the most beneficial features of E-Z Rules, and we strongly recommend it.

ROADMAP TO ARTICLE 9

Special Cases:

I. THE SECURITY INTEREST

OVERVIEW

- UCC Article 9 covers any transaction "*Substantively a Security Interest*"
- In order to determine whether a transaction is "*Substantively a Security Interest*," the UCC directs us to look at **Substance over Form** (§1-201(37)).
- Actual Intent of Parties is often considered.
- The Property Interest:
  - A Lien is a Property Interest (thus, a S/I must attach to the property).
  - A Secured Pty has a *Contingent Future Interest*, in property subject to a lien, contingent on the Debtor's default of the Debtor's obligation (which is secured by the collateral under the S/A).
  - Other property interests arise with Leases and Consignments:
    - In a "*True Lease*" the lessor owns the property and leases it to the lessee; since the lessor owns it, the property is not subject to the lessee's creditors.
    - Many Creditors attempt to disguise transactions as leases so that the property will also not be subject to the "Lessee's" creditors. In such a transaction, the Creditor steps into the lessor's shoes (and the Debtor steps into the lessee's shoes). Since §1-201(37) dictates that we look to *Substance over Form*, however, we would consider the "lessor" to be a Creditor and the property which purports to be leased as ordinary "collateral" - owned by the debtor (For more detail, see discussion below on Leases and Consignments, under "Special Cases").

- It is important to determine what type of property interest the Creditor has when dealing with the following issues:
  - **Default:** If Debtor goes into default
    - Remedy is Disposition (as per Part 5 of Article 9) if the transaction is considered to be a Secured Transaction
    - Remedy is Repossession/Replevin if the transaction is considered to be a "Consignment" or "True Lease"
  - **Purchasers:** S/I holders take subject to Bona-Fide purchasers; property owners (i.e. lessors/consignors) do not.

RELEVANT RULES: 1-201(37); 9-102; 9-104

§1-201(37): The Security Interest:

a) A **"Security Interest"** ("S/I") is:

1. An interest in personal property or fixtures which *secures payment or performance* of an obligation.

or 2. Any interest of a buyer of Accounts or Chattel Paper which is subject to Article 9 (under §9-106, §9-105(b), and §9-104(f)).

b) The effect of a *retention* or *reservation* of Title by the seller (in the collateral) is limited to a reservation of a S/I (even if shipped and delivered pursuant to §2-401).

c) The property interest granted in §2-401 (when a seller identifies goods intended for buyer) is not a S/I, *unless* the requirements of Article 9 are met (i.e. attachment and perfection).

d) **Consignment** - the reservation of title in a consignment is <u>not</u> a S/I unless it is *intended* to be a Security Interest (subject to §2-326).

e) **Leases**

1. Look at the <u>facts of each case</u> to determine if a transaction creates a lease or a S/I.
2. A S/I is created if the consideration for the lease is
   - i) <u>For the term of the lease</u> (Not subject to termination by the Lessee)
   - and ii) <u>*Either:*</u>
     - (a) The original term of the lease is ≥ the remaining economic life of the goods.
     - or (b) The Lessee is <u>required</u> to *either:*
       - 1) Renew the lease for the remaining economic life
       - or 2) Buy the goods
     - or (c) The Lessee has an <u>Option to Renew</u> the lease for the remaining economic life of the goods for *either:*
       - 1) No Additional Consideration
       - or 2) Nominal Consideration
     - or (d) The Lessee has the <u>Option to Buy</u> the goods for *either:*
       - 1) No additional Consideration
       - or 2) Nominal Consideration

3. A transaction will <u>not</u> necessarily be considered a S/I if it merely provides that:
   - (a) The PV of the consideration (rent) is *substantially* ≥ the FMV of the goods at the time of entering into the lease agreement.
   - or (b) The Lessee:
     1. Assume Risk of Loss
     - or 2. Pays Taxes, Insurance, Filing, Recording, and Registration Fees
     - or 3. Pays for Service and/or Maintenance of goods
   - or (c) The Lessee has the option to Renew the lease or Buy goods.
   - or (d) The Lessee has the option to Renew the lease for a Fixed rent the *reasonably predictable* FMV of rent at the time of the option
   - or (e) The Lessee has an option to Buy goods for a Fixed Price ≥ the *reasonably predictable* FMV of goods at time of option.

4. **Definitions:**

(x) **"Nominal Consideration"** -

1) Consideration is NOT Nominal if:

(i) The renewal rent is the FMV at the time of the option.

or (ii) The Purchase price is the FMV at the time of the option.

2) Consideration IS Nominal if it is < the lessee's reasonably predicted cost of performing under the lease (if option isn't exercised)

(y) **"Reasonably Predictable"** and **"Remaining Economic Life"** are to be determined with reference to the *facts and circumstances* at the time transaction is entered into.

(z) **"Present Value"** (the amount of future payments discounted to a certain date):

1) The Discount Rate is determined by the interest rate specified by the parties (if reasonable)

2) If there is no rate in agreement, the interest rate = the *Commercially Reasonable Rate* that would be applied in a similar the situation (under the circumstances).

§9-102: Policy & Subject Of Article 9

(1) Except as provided in §9-104, Article 9 applies to:

(a) Any transaction *intended to create a Security Interest* (regardless of form) in Personal Property or Fixtures, including:

1. Goods
or 2. Documents
or 3. Instruments
or 4. General Intangibles
or 5. Chattel paper
or 6. Accounts

and (b) Any sale of Accounts or Chattel Paper

(2) Article 9 also applies to Security Interests made by Contract, including:

a. Pledges
and b. Assignments
and c. Chattel Mortgages/Trusts
and d. Conditional Sales
and e. Trust Receipts
and f. Factor's Liens
and g. Trust Deeds
and h. Equipment Trusts
and i. Liens (NOT Statutory liens, unless provided for in §9-310)
and j. Title Retention Contracts
and k. Leases or Consignments Intended as a Security Interest (see §1-201(37))

(3) The application of this Article is not affected by the fact that an obligation is secured by a transaction or interest which this Article does not apply to.

§9-104: Transactions Excluded From Article 9:

This Article does NOT apply to:

(a) A S/I subject to any **U.S. Statute** governing the rights of parties (including Third Pty) affected by transactions in particular types of property.

(b) To a **Landlord's Lien**

(c) To a **Statutory Lien** or Lien for services or materials (unless allowed under §9-310)

(d) To a **Transfer of a Claim for Employee Compensation** (including wages and salary)

(e) To a **Transfer by a Government** or government agency

(f) To the **Sale of Accounts or Chattel Paper** if:

1. They are part of a Sale of the Business from which they originated

or 2. They are an *Assignment* for the purpose of Collection ONLY

or 3. They are a Transfer of a Right to Payment to an Assignee who is also obligated to perform under the contract

or 4. They are a transfer of a Single Account to an Assignee in satisfaction (in whole or in part) of a preexisting debt

(g) To a **Transfer of an Interest in an Insurance Policy**, unless provided for in:

1. §9-306 (Insurance is a Proceed)

and 2. §9-312 (Priorities in Proceeds)

(h) To a **Right represented by a judgment** (unless judgment is on collateral)

(i) Any **Right of Set-off**

(j) **Real Estate Transactions** including:

1. The Creation of an Lien or interest in Real Estate
2. The Transfer of an Lien or interest in Real Estate
3. Any leases or rents thereunder

(k) To a **Transfer of any Tort Claim**

(l) A **Transfer of Interest in a Deposit Account** (as per §9-105(1)) unless: they are proceeds and provided for in:

1. §9-306 (general proceeds rules)

or 2. §9-312 (priority in proceeds)

II. ATTACHMENT

1. ATTACHING THE SECURITY INTEREST

OVERVIEW

- **Attachment** is created with a Security Agreement between the two parties
- **Perfection** occurs when the Creditor puts the *rest of the world* on Notice (by filing or possession)
- A Security Agreement ("S/A") may be created in 2 ways:
  - **Orally** - Must be accompanied by Possession

  or
  - **In Writing** - Usually must be accompanied by Possession or Filing
- Filing may occur before attachment (thus, perfection occurs upon attachment)
- **Debtor's Rights in Collateral**: §9-203(1)(c) requires Debtor to have rights in collateral for attachment; Thus, attachment on After-Acquired property occurs only when the new collateral becomes debtor's property.
- Automatic Attachment occurs with After-acquired Property covered by a valid S/A
- **Requirements For Attachment** (§9-203 (see below)):
  - AGREEMENT for S/I to attach (Possession or Writing)
  - VALUE must be given
  - Debtor has a RIGHTS to Collateral

RELEVANT RULES: 9-203

§9-203: Attachment And Enforceability Of Security Interest:

(1) **Requirements for Attachment**:

i) A Security Interest Attaches ONLY If:

(a) The collateral is **Secured** with *either:*

1. **Possession:** In the Possession of the Secured Pty (pursuant to agreement)

or 2. **Security Agreement:** Debtor has signed a Security Agreement which:

a. Is in WRITING

and b. Describes the Collateral (as per §9-110)

(Note: When collateral is crops or timber, a description of the land is required)

or 3. **Control of Investment Property** - If:

a. The collateral is INVENTMENT PROPERTY

and b. The Secured Pty has Control over the Investment Property (as per §9-115(1)(e))

and c. The Secured Paarty is Controlling it pursuant to an agreement

and (b) **Value** has been given

and (c) **Debtor's Rights:** The Debtor has Rights in the collateral

ii) Requirements are subject to

a) §4-208 for Security Interests of a Collecting Bank

b) §9-115 and §9-116 for Security Interests in Investment Property

c) §9-113 for Security Interests arising under the Article of Sales (Article 2)

(2) **Time of Attachment**: A Security Interest attaches:

a) When it becomes enforceable against the Debtor (with respect to the collateral)

and b) *Either:*

i) As soon as the events specified in (1) take place **(they Must Coexist)**

or ii) When agreed (if agreement explicitly postpones the time of attachment)

(3) **Rights to Proceeds**: Secured Pty has the rights to Proceeds under §9-306 (i.e. no need to specify that proceeds will be covered by the S/A, unless otherwise agreed. You usually must specify if you do <u>not</u> want proceeds to be covered by the S/A).

(4) Transactions subject to this article are also subject to other statutes; those statutes shall supersede this article (ex: small loans, retail installment selling statutes, etc.).

2. *REQUIREMENT 1: WRITING (The Security Agreement)*

OVERVIEW

- The Security Agreement can be created in two ways
  - Orally - Must be accompanied by Possession
  - or In Writing - Usually must be accompanied by Possession or Filing
- Requirements of the Written S/A: (See §9-203(1)(i)(a)2.)
  - Must be Signed by Debtor (no need for Creditor's signature)
  - and Must contain a Description of the collateral
  - and Must Grant a S/I, *either with*:
    - Language granting Creditor a S/I in collateral
    - or Parole Evidence indicating a Grant (if there is no such clause in the S/A)
- Description of Collateral: (see §9-110)
  - The S/A is only required to describe the collateral generally, yet it must be detailed enough for a Third Pty to "*reasonably identify*" the collateral.
  - It is Best to describe collateral in more general terms, so one can obtain a S/I in the greatest amount of items.
  - Minor errors are not a problem, as long as the "*reasonably identifiable*" standard is fulfilled.
  - Other Details:
    - *After-Acquired Property* - Must be specified to be covered by the S/A
    - *Future Advances* - Must be specified to be covered by the S/A
    - *Proceeds* - Do not have to be specified for inclusion

- Using the Financing Statement as a S/A
  - Usually a F/S is not good enough to be used as a S/A (although people often file a F/S before the S/A is finalized for faster perfection)
  - A F/S may be used as a S/A if it contains the requirements of a S/A
  - One may often use a S/A as a F/S, however

RELEVANT RULES: 9-201; 9-110

§9-201: General Validity Of Security Agreement:

1. A Security Agreement is effective according to its terms:
   a) Between the parties
   and b) Against purchasers of the collateral
   and c) Against creditors (i.e. other than a S/P)
   and d) Except as otherwise provided by the UCC

2. This Article Does Not:
   a) Validate illegal practices or charges (governed by statutes or regulations regarding usury, small loans, retail installment sales, or the like).
   b) Extend the application of any such statute or regulation to any transaction not otherwise subject to this Article.

§9-110: Sufficiency Of Description:

Description of Personal or Real Property need not be specific if it *reasonably identifies* what is described.

3. *REQUIREMENT 2: VALUE*

OVERVIEW

- §9-201(1)(b) requires value to be given (in exchange for the S/I) for attachment to occur.
- The value requirement will be fulfilled if a S/I is given:
  - In return for consideration
  - or As Security for a Preexisting Claim (ex: after-acquired property clause)
  - or As partial or total **Satisfaction** of an existing claim (ex: security agreement made before any collateral was available (see §9-108 above))
  - or In return for a Binding Commitment to extend credit
- Value for After-Acquired Property - Note: when Inventory or Floating Liens are secured, they are classified as being "**In the Ordinary Course Of Business**," and are deemed to have value.

RELEVANT RULES: 1-201(44)

§1-201(44): Value:

1) A Person is deemed to give "**Value**" if he acquires his rights *either:*
   (a) In return for *either:*
      1. A Binding Commitment to **Extend Credit** (ex: L/C)
      or 2. An Extension of **Immediately Available Credit**
   or (b) A Security for total or partial **Satisfaction** of a pre-existing claim
   or (c) By accepting delivery pursuant to a pre-existing contract for purchase
   or (d) In return for any "sufficient" consideration (as would support a simple contract)
2) This section is subject to:
   a) §3-303: Negotiable Instruments
   b) §4-208; §4-209: Bank Collections

4. REQUIREMENT 3: DEBTOR'S RIGHTS IN COLLATERAL

OVERVIEW

- §9-203(1)(c) requires Debtor to have rights in collateral for attachment to occur.
- Title of collateral is irrelevant, as the UCC looks to Substance over Form (see 1-201(37))
- Debtor must have an "*ownership interests or right to obtain possession*" for attachment to occur
- Debtor normally obtains rights in goods when "*they have been IDENTIFIED by the seller as intended for the buyer*" (see §2-501)
- This is important, because if the collateral is already covered by a perfected S/A (which is reflected by a filed F/S), then attachment occurs at the time the Debtor obtains rights in the collateral.

5. *AFTER-ACQUIRED PROPERTY:*

OVERVIEW

- The S/A must specifically mention that After-Acquired Property is will be covered (§9-204)
- Perfection will automatically occur when the Debtor receives rights (i.e. the goods are attached) in the After-Acquired property if the original S/A was already filed (§9-203(1) and §9-303(1)).

- Special Cases:
    - **Consumer Goods:** A S/A can only cover After-Acquired property for goods acquired within 10 Days after the S/A was created.
    - **Household Goods:** A S/A cannot cover After-Acquired Household goods.
    - **Inventory:** When taking a S/I in inventory there is NO need to Specify after-acquired inventory" (it is assumed).
    - **"Floating Liens"** (accounts, intangibles, etc.) - Like inventory, it need not be specified to include After-Acquired Property.

RELEVANT RULES: 9-108; 9-204

§9-108: After-Acquired Property:

The S/I in the After-Acquired Property will be considered to have been taken for *New Value* (i.e. not as a Security for an Antecedent (prior) Debt) if:

a) The Secured Pty secures the After-Acquired Property by *either:*
- 1) Making an Advance
- or 2) Incurring an Obligation
- or 3) Releasing an already Perfected S/I
- or 4) Otherwise giving "New Value"

and b) The Debtor acquires rights in collateral *either:*
- 1) In the **Ordinary Course of Business**
- or 2) Under a **Contract of Purchase** made:
  - a. Pursuant to the S/A
  - and b. Within a reasonable time after *new value is given*

§9-204(1),(2): After-Acquired Property:

(1) A S/A may provide for After-Acquired Property to secure the obligations covered by the S/A (except as provided below in (2)).

(2) **Consumer Goods Exception:**

a) After-Acquired Property will not attach to a S/I if:
- 1. The S/I is in Consumer Goods
- and 2. The After-Acquired Property is given as *additional* security

b) Exceptions: After-Acquired Property will attach in Consumer Goods if:
- 1. Debtor acquires rights in the After-Acquired Property within 10 Days after the Secured Pty gave value
- or 2. They are Accessions (see §9-314)

III. PERFECTION

1. PERFECTING THE SECURITY INTEREST

OVERVIEW

- Perfection generally occurs when a S/I in Personal property cannot be defeated by other creditors or in an insolvency proceeding.
- Perfection closes off the rights off other subsequent creditors to priority in the collateral (except for PMSI holders).
- There must be a point in time where the collateral is both **Attached** ***and*** **Perfected**
- Perfection can occur in numerous ways:
  - Security Agreement + Filing (a.k.a. "Hypothecation") (not good for money/instruments) (see FILING below)
  - Security Agreement + Possession (a.k.a. "Pledge") (not good for most intangibles) (See POSSESSION below)
    - *Actual possession of goods*
    - *Possession of Negotiable Document*
  - Security Agreement + Notation on Certificate of Title (for motor vehicles; titled goods)
  - Automatic Perfection - Only Security Agreement (see AUTOMATIC PERFECTION below)
    - **PMSI** in Consumer Goods (§9-302(1)(d))
    - Qualifying **Proceeds** (§9-306(3))
    - **After-Acquired Property** - already covered by a perfected S/I (§9-204(1))
    - **Beneficial Interests** (§9-4302(1)(c))
    - **Assignment** of Accounts (§9-302(1)(e))
  - Control of **Investment Property** - Security Agreement not needed (see §9-115 and §9-116)

- Temporary-Automatic Perfection (see also TEMPORARY AUTOMATIC PERFECTION)
    - Instruments - 21 Days (§9-304(4))
    - Certificated Securities - 21 Days (§9-304(4))
    - Certain Negotiable Documents - 21 Days (§9-304(4))
    - PMSIs - 10 Days (§9-301(2))
    - Proceeds - 10 Days (§9-306(3)(c))

RELEVANT RULES: 9-303; 9-304; 9-308

§9-303: Perfection:

(1) A S/I is Perfected when it has Attached to the collateral AND either
a) All of the required steps for perfection have been taken as specified in *either:*
1. §9-302 (Perfection by Filing)
or 2. §9-304 (Perfection of Instruments)
or 3. §9-305 (Perfection by Possession)
or 4. §9-306 (Perfection in Proceeds)
or 5. §9-115 (Investment Property)
or b) If the required steps (above) are taken before attachment, the Security Interest attaches

(2) **Continuous Perfection**: The S/I shall be deemed to be Perfected Continuously (for purposes of Article 9) if:
a) A S/I is originally perfected in any way (permitted under Article 9)
and b) The S/I is *subsequently* perfected (renewed) in some other way (under Article 9)
and c) There was no intermediate time when the S/I was not perfected

§9-304: Perfection Of Instruments:

(1) Perfecting Instruments

a) A S/I in Chattel Paper or Negotiable Documents may be perfected by filing.

b) A S/I in Money or Instruments (other than chattel paper) can only be perfected by **Possession** *unless:*

1) It is an Instrument which is **temporarily perfected** under §9-304(4) or (5)

2) It is Proceeds, which is **temporarily perfected** under §9-306(2) or (3)

(2) Perfecting Documents of Goods

a) When goods are in the possession of an issuer of a Negotiable Document (representing the goods), the Goods may be perfected by perfecting a S/I in the document.

b) Any other S/I in the goods (i.e. perfected in any other way) will be subject to the S/I in the document

(3) Perfecting Permissive Filings

a) If Goods are in the possession of a *Bailee* (other than the issuer of a Negotiable Document), they may be perfected by *either:*

1) The issuance of a Document in the name of the Secured Pty

or 2) A Receipt by the Bailee with a *notification* of the Secured Pty's interest

or 3) By filing as to the goods

b) If a Bailee has issued a Negotiable Document for the goods, §9-304(2) applies.

(4) Temporary Perfection Without Filing

a) A S/I is automatically perfected for 21 Days from the time of **attachment** (even without proper filing or possession) for:

1) Instruments

and 2) Negotiable Documents (only includes goods in a Bailee's possession if it made a Negotiable Document for those goods)

and 3) Certificated Securities

b) Requirements for Automatic Temporary perfection:

1) The S/I must arise under a *written* Security Agreement

and 2) *New value* must be given for the S/I

(5) Continued Perfection when Collateral is Given to Debtor

A S/I remains perfected for 21 Days (without filing) if

1) A Secured Pty has a Perfected S/I in:

a) An Instrument

or b) A Negotiable Document

or c) Goods in the possession of a Bailee

or d) Certificated Security

and 2) The S/P has:

(a) Made available Goods or Documents to the Debtor for the purpose of:

1) Ultimate Sale or Exchange

or 2) Loading/Unloading/Storing

or 3) Shipping/Transshipping

or 4) Manufacturing/Processing

or 5) Dealing with them in a manner preliminary to sale/exchange

**** Note: Priority between conflicting S/I's in goods are subject to §9-312(3)

or (b) Delivered Instruments or Cetrtificated Securities to the Debtor for the purpose of:

1) Ultimate sale or exchange

or 2) Presentation (for sale)

or 3) Collection

or 4) Renewal

or 5) Registration of Transfer

(6) After the 21 Day Period, the S/I must be perfected by complying with the applicable provisions in Article 9 if:

a) It is still not perfected (as per (4))

or b) It is still in debtor's possession (as per (5))

§9-308: Chattel Paper and Instruments:

Purchasers of Chattel Paper or Instruments take Priority over a S/I in that Chattel Paper or Instrument if the purchaser takes it:

(a) **Without Knowledge of S/I**: To maintain priority, the Purchaser must prove that:

1. Purchaser took *without knowledge* that the Chattel Paper or Instrument is subject to a S/I

and 2. New Value was given for it

and 3. He took Possession of the Chattel Paper in the Ordinary Course of his Business

and 4. It is Perfected under *either:*

a) §9-304 (permissive filing and temporary perfection)

or b) §9-306 (perfection as to proceeds)

or (b) **With Knowledge**: To maintain priority, the Purchaser must prove that:

1. The Instrument or Chattel Paper is *Proceeds of Inventory*, subject to a S/I (as per §9-306) even though he knows that the specific Chattel Paper or Instrument. is subject to a S/I

and 2. New Value was given for it

and 3. He took Possession of the Chattel Paper in the *Ordinary Course of his Business*

2. PERFECTING WITH POSSESSION

OVERVIEW

- A person cannot perfect with Possession for Intangibles (ex: accounts, securities)
- Goods in possession of a Bailee - may be perfected by:
  - **Possession of a Negotiable Receipt** - possession of a Negotiable Instrument (which is written by the Bailee of the goods,) representing goods/inventory, is considered to be the equivalent of possession of those goods.
  - or **Notification** - the Creditor is considered to have possession of the collateral once he notifies the Bailee (of the goods) that he is now the holder of a S/I in those goods.
  - or **Filing a Financing Statement** - this is the safest method
- Goods Placed in Escrow: There is a conflict as to whether placing goods in an Escrow account is considered possession:
  - Not considered possession - Dolly Madison
  - Considered possession if the collateral is not in control of Debtor - In re Copeland
- Negotiable Receipts & Field Warehousing:
  - Negotiable receipts are created when a S/P wants to take a S/I in goods placed in a warehouse, or with a Bailee (a.k.a. "Field Warehousing")
  - A person who takes a Negotiable Receipt by **Due Negotiation** takes FREE of any S/I (filing is thus, ineffective with Negotiable Instruments and Promissory Notes)
  - The words "*to the order of*" usually makes a document negotiable

RELEVANT RULES: 9-305

§9-305: Perfecting By Possession:

1) Possession may be used to perfect a S/I in:
a) Letters of Credit (as per §5-116)
or b) Goods
or c) Instruments (other than certified securities)
or d) Money
or e) Negotiable Documents
or f) Chattel Paper

2) **Time of Possession with Bailee**: If Collateral is held by a Bailee, the Secured Pty is deemed to have possession when the Bailee *receives notification* of the Secured Pty's interest (unless the Bailee issues a Negotiable Document for the goods).

3) Perfection begins at the time of Possession (No Relation Back), and *continues* only as long as possession is retained (unless otherwise specified in UCC (ex: §9-304(5)'s 21 Day rule)).

4) The S/I can otherwise be Perfected Before or After possession only as provided by other sections of the UCC.

A. *Effectiveness of Perfection by Possession*

OVERVIEW

- Perfection (by possession) begins upon Possession
- Perfection continues only while collateral *remains* in possession unless it falls under the exceptions in §9-304 (see below)

§9-304(5)-(6): Perfection Of Instruments:

(5) Continued Perfection when Collateral is Given to Debtor

A S/I remains perfected for 21 Days (without filing) if

1) A Secured Pty has a Perfected S/I in:

a) An Instrument

or b) A Negotiable Document

or c) Goods in the possession of a Bailee

or d) A Certificated Security

and 2) The S/P has:

(a) Made available Goods or Documents to the Debtor for the purpose of:

1) Ultimate Sale or Exchange

or 2) Loading/Unloading/Storing

or 3) Shipping/Transshipping

or 4) Manufacturing/Processing

or 5) Dealing with them in a manner preliminary to sale/exchange

**** Note: Priority between conflicting S/I's in goods are subject to §9-312(3)

or (b) Delivered Instruments or Certificated Securites to the Debtor for the purpose of:

1) Ultimate sale or exchange

or 2) Presentation (for sale)

or 3) Collection

or 4) Renewal

or 5) Registration of Transfer

(6) After the 21 Day Period, the S/I must be perfected by complying with the applicable provisions in Article 9 if:

a) It is still not perfected (as per (4))

or b) It is still in debtor's possession (as per (5))

B. Secured Party's Duties and Rights in Possession

(§9-207)

OVERVIEW

- A S/P has the following Rights and Duties to the Debtor, while she keeps the collateral in her possession:
  - a) Duty of Reasonable Care
  - b) Duty to Notify Debtor - if anything must be done to collateral (ex: repairs)
  - c) Duty to Account for Rents - S/P must give Debtor any rent money collected from collateral
  - d) Duty to Insure - S/P must insure goods, yet Debtor must pay excess loss which insurance does not cover
  - c) Right to Use Collateral - S/P may use collateral if it does not diminish its value.
  - f) Right to Reimburse - S/P may charge Debtor reasonable possession expenses (ex: insurance, storage, etc.)

* For more detail see "Rights of Parties" below

RELEVANT RULES: 9-207

§9-207: Secured Party's Rights And Duties Over Collateral In Its Possession:

(1) **Secured Parties Obligation:**

a) **General Collateral:** A S/P must use *Reasonable Care* in the custody and preservation of the collateral in its possession.

b) **Instruments and Chattel Paper**: *Reasonable Care* includes taking the necessary steps to preserve rights against prior parties (unless otherwise agreed).

(2) **Rights and Duties of the S/P:** Unless parties otherwise agree, the following rights and duties apply when the S/P has Possession of the collateral:

(a) Reasonable Expectations: A Secured Pty may charge the Debtor (and be secured for) any *Reasonable Expenses* (including insurance, taxes, and other charges) incurred in the:

1. Custody of the collateral
or 2. Preservation of the collateral
or 3. Operation/use of the collateral

(b) Risk of Loss: If Insurance proceeds are insufficient, the Debtor shall bear the risk of Accidental Loss or Damage of the collateral.

(c) Value from the Collateral:

1. **Non-Monetary:** The S/P may hold any increase in value or profits (except money) received from the collateral as additional security for the debt.
2. **Money:** Money received from the collateral (as profits from its increased value) shall *either* be:
   a) Returned to the Debtor
   or b) Applied in reduction of the secured debt

(d) Identification of Collateral: If the collateral is not fungible, the S/P must keep it *identifiable* (fungible property may be commingled (ex: grain)).

(e) Re-pledging: The S/P may re-pledge the collateral if it does not impair the debtor's rights to redeem it.

(3) Although the S/P will be liable for any loss caused by his failure to comply with the above obligations, he will not lose his S/I.

(4) **Use of Collateral:** A S/P may use or operate the collateral if it is:

a) For the purpose of preserving the collateral or its value
or b) Pursuant to a court order (in the appropriate jurisdiction)
or c) To the extent provided in the S/A (unless it's a Consumer Good)

3. *PERFECTION BY FILING*

A. *How to File:*

OVERVIEW

- Filing effectiveness lasts for **5 Yrs**. (§9-403(2))
- A filed F/S must be renewed within **6 months** before the 5 yr. period expires (§9-403(3)).
- Renewal may be done by either:
  - Filing a Continuation Statement
  - or Re-filing a new F/S
- Filing will be effective upon presentation of the F/S to the Filing Officer (§9-403(1))

RELEVANT RULES: 9-403; 9-407

§9-403: Filing Process:

(1) Filing occurs upon:

a) Presentation of a F/S for filing

and b) *Either:*

1) Tendering the filing fee

or 2) Accepting the F/S by the Filing Officer

(2) Duration of Filing:

a) A filed F/S is effective for 5 Yrs. from the date of filing (subject to (6) below).

b) A Continuation Statement must be filed *before expiration* of the term (5 Yrs.) in order to continue perfection (i.e. the F/S's effectiveness)

c) If an Insolvency Proceeding occurs, the F/S will be effective until the *later* of:
1. The expiration of the 5 Yr. filing period
or 2. 60 days after the proceedings have terminated

d) Upon lapse, the S/I becomes Unperfected, *unless* it is perfected without filing (ex: by possession).

e) A S/I which becomes unperfected due to lapse, is deemed to have always been unperfected when dealing with a person who became a Lien Creditor or a Purchaser *before* it lapsed.

(3) **The Continuation Statement**

a) A Continuation Statement (C/S) may be filed by a Secured Pty within 6 Mos. *prior to* the expiration of the 5 Yr. period

b) **Requirements of a Continuation Statement:**
1. Be signed by Secured Pty
and 2. Identify the original F/S by file #
and 3. State that the original statement is still effective

c) A C/S which is signed by a person who is not a Secured Pty must
1. Be accompanied by a written statement of assignment (complying with §9-405(2)), signed by Secured Pty
and 2. Include payment of the required fee

d) Upon filing of the C/S, the Perfection period is extended for another 5 Yrs. (from the date of expiration (not 5 Yrs from filing of the C/S))

e) Subsequent C/S's may be filed (in the same manner) to continue perfection

f) A F/S may be removed or destroyed if
1. It has expired over a year ago
or 2. It is preserved on microfilm (or other photographic record)

(4) Duties of the Filing Officer: (subject to (7) below) A Filing Officer shall:
a. Mark each statement with an assigned file # and time of filing
and b. Retain a copy of it on record or on microfilm *for public inspection*
and c. Index the F/S by Debtor's name (indicating the file # and address of Debtor in index)

(5) Filing Fee * * *
(Note: there is usually a higher fee for filing a non-standard F/S form (i.e. filing the S/A as the F/S))

(6) Exceptions to 5 Yr. Perfection Period:
a) If Debtor is a Transmitting Utility (pursuant to §9-401(5)), the F/S may allow perfection to remain effective until a Termination Statement is filed
b) A Mortgage filed as a Fixture Filing (as per §9-402(6)) is effective until:
1. The mortgage is released or satisfied
or 2. Its effectiveness otherwise terminates as to the real estate

(7) Indexing Records
a) The Filing Officer shall index the F/S in the same manner as mortgages are indexed (as if the Debtor and S/P were a mortgagor and mortgagee respectively) for collateral consisting of:
1) Natural Resources
2) Accounts subject to §9-103(5)
3) Fixture Financing Statement (as per §9-313) for goods to become fixtures

b) If a state requires, the F/S shall be indexed under
1) The Debtor's name (as if he were the mortgagor)
and 2) The Secured Pty's name (as if he were a mortgagee)

§9-407: Information From Filing Officer:
(*optional provision*)

(1) Upon request, the Filing Officer shall give the person filing the F/S a copy of it, with the filing time and date stamped on it (this rule shall also apply to Statement of Assignment, Termination Statement, and Statement of Release).

(2) Upon request of any person, the Filing Officer shall issue a Certificate showing whether there is any effective F/S naming a particular Debtor, and the time and date on which each F/S was filed.

B. When to File:

RELEVANT RULE: 9-302

§9-302: When Filing Is Not Required:

(1) A **Financing Statement** **MUST BE FILED** to perfect all S/I's, **UNLESS** it is:

(a) A S/I in Collateral which is already **in Possession** of the Secured Pty (pursuant to §9-305)

or (b) A S/I **temporarily perfected,** *either:*

1. In instruments, documents, or certified securities without delivery (as per §9-304 - 21 Day rule and §9-115 - Controlrule)

or 2. In proceeds for a 10 Day period (as per §9-306)

or (c) A S/I created by an Assignment of a Beneficial Interest in a Trust (or a decedents estate)

or (d) **A PMSI in CONSUMER GOODS,** unless it is for

1. Motor Vehicles required to be registered

or 2. Fixtures (as per §9-313)

or (e) An **Assignment of Accounts,** which does not transfer a significant part of the assignor's accounts (alone or in conjunction with other assignments to the same Assignee)

or (f) A S/I

1. Of a Collecting Bank (§4-208)

or 2. Arising under Article 2 (Article on Sales) (as per §9-113)

or 3. Covered in (3) below

or (g) **An Assignment:**

1. For the benefit of all creditors of the transferor

and 2. Subsequent transfers by the Assignee

or (h) **An Investment Property:**

1. The Security Interest is in Investment Property

and 2. It is perfected without filing (as per §9-115 or §9-116)

(2) If a Perfected S/I is assigned, re-filing is not required to continue perfection against the original debtor's creditors.

(3) Filing is NOT Required to perfect a S/I in property already subject to:

(a) **A U.S. Statute/Treaty** providing for

1. International/national Registration

or 2. An international/national Certificate of Title

or 3. A specific place of filing (different than UCC)

or (b) **A Certificate of Title Statute** or **Central Filing Statute,** *unless* the collateral is **Inventory** held by a *"Merchant"* (a person in the business of selling those kinds of goods) - in which UCC filing (as per Part 4) applies

or (c) A Certificate of Title statute (of another jurisdiction) requiring that the S/I be stated on the certificate to be perfected (ex: automobiles).

(4) When complying with any statute/treaty in (3), a S/I will be subject to the UCC in *all but the following areas:*

a) Filing pursuant to a statute - will be equivalent to filing a financing statement under Article 9

b) Perfection - will be subject to those particular statutes, except as provided in §9-103 for Multi-State transactions

c) Duration/Renewal of perfection - will be governed by the statute

C. What to File: The Financing Statement

OVERVIEW

- Name and Address of Secured Pty - must be specific enough for someone to identify and contact S/P for more information
- Debtor's Name:
    - Debtor must be identified by its REAL Name
    - Partnerships - Debtor's name OK; Partnership name okay
    - Trade names - not adequate alone - must also put real name
    - Changing Name (or Structure, See §9-402(7))
    - Changing Address/Location (See §9-401(3))
- Best to check Corporate Charter for real name of the Debtor
- Failure to fix a changed name, address, etc. of Debtor does not affect the S/I in the perfected collateral; only collateral obtained *after* the change (+ any leeway time (ex: 4 months)) will be deemed unperfected (until the F/S is changed to reflect the correct name of the Debtor)
- **When Debtor Moves to another State:** See §9-103 for re-filing instructions if Debtor moves to another state.
- **Change of use** - in collateral is usually immaterial, re-filing is usually not required (See §9-401).
- The F/S need not specify After-Acquired Property (although the S/A must specify it) as long as the description in the F/S covers the type of property (which the After-Acquired Property can be classified under)

- **The Signature of Debtor** is normally required:
    - It can be typed as long as Debtor's intent is obvious.
    - **Exceptions:** If Debtor does not sign the F/S in the following cases, the filing *will still be effective if* (see §9-402(2)):
        - The Collateral is acquired after Debtor changes name or identity of Company (and F/S is changed)
        - The S/P re-filed the F/S because Debtor moved, or his collateral has moved
        - The Collateral is Proceeds (requiring a new filing)
        - Re-filing the F/S to extend the time frame of its effectiveness (ex: before or after 5 yr. expiration)
- Amendments:
    - Must be signed by BOTH parties
    - If the Amendment adds new collateral, the effective date (for the new collateral covered) is upon filing of Amendment (i.e. it does not "relate back" to the filing of the original F/S)
- Description - may be more general than in the S/A, since a S/P is expected to be more cautious and investigate the F/S further.

RELEVANT RULES: 9-402

§9-402: The Financing Statement:

(1) **Requirements of a Financing Statement:**

a) Required Contents:

1) Signatures, Names and Addresses of Debtors
and 2) Names of Secured Parties
and 3) Address of Secured Pty who can supply information about the S/I (to others)
and 4) Description of Collateral, *either*
a. Describing the items of collateral
or b. Indicating the types of collateral
and 5) Additional details of collateral required:
a. Description of Real Estate - for Crops
b. Must comply with§9-402(5) for
1. Natural Resources (oil, gas, minerals, timber)
2. Accounts subject to §9-103(5)
3. Fixture Financing Statement (as per §9-313) for goods which are (or will become) fixtures

b) A Financing Statement may be filed *before*:
1) A Security Agreement is made
or 2) A S/I otherwise Attaches

c) **Using a Security Agreement as a Financing Statement:**
1) A copy of the Security Agreement can serve as a valid Financing Statement if:
a. It contains the above information (in (1))
and b. It is signed by the Debtor
2) A photocopy or carbon copy of the Security Agreement is also valid (as a Financing Statement) if:
a. The Security Agreement allows
or b. The original had been filed in the state

(2) **Absence of Debtor's Signature:** A Financing Statement (complying with (1) (above)) signed by the Secured Pty but not the Debtor is only sufficient to perfect a S/I in:

(a) Collateral which is/was already subject to a S/I in <u>another jurisdiction</u> when:

1. It is brought into the state

or 2. Debtor's location is changed to that state

(*** Note: Financing Statement must say that the collateral was brought into this state or that the Debtor's location was changed to this state under such circumstances)

or (b) <u>Proceeds</u> under §9-306 if the S/I in the original collateral was perfected.

(*** Note: Financing Statement Must describe original collateral)

or (c) Collateral as to which <u>filing has lapsed</u> (Note: The S/P Must be re-file)

or (d) Collateral acquired after <u>Debtor changed his Name, Identity, or Corporate Structure</u>

(3) Complying Financing Statement Form * * *

(For detail see model format in statute; see also "UCC Form 1" financing statement)

(4) <u>Amending the Financing Statement:</u>

a) F/S may be amended by filing an amendment which is:

1. In <u>Writing</u>

and 2. <u>Signed</u> by both the Debtor and Secured Pty

b) Amendments do not extend the period of the F/S's effectiveness

c) Amendments adding collateral are effective as of the filing date of the amendment (i.e. perfection date for priority purposes is NOT the original perfection date for the new collateral)

d) Whenever "Financing Statement" is referred to (in Article 9), it includes the original F/S and all amendments.

(5) Financing Statements Requiring Real Estate Description:

1) Financing Statements must describe Real Estate for collateral of
   - a) Natural Resources (oil, gas, minerals, timber)
   - b) Accounts subject to §9-103(5)
   - c) Fixture Financing Statement (as per §9-313) for goods which are (or will become) fixtures

2) F/S Requirements:
   - a) Show that it covers this type of collateral
   - and b) Recite that it is filed in the Real Estate records
   - and c) Give enough detail of the Real Property -sufficient to give Constructive Notice of the mortgage or Real Property (pursuant to the state law)

3) If the Debtor does not have an interest of record in the land then F/S must show the name of a "record owner" (of the property)

(6) Fixture Filing Mortgages:

i) A Mortgage is effective as a F/S for Fixture Filings from the date of its recording if:
   - (a) The goods are described in the mortgage by item or type
   - and (b) The goods are to become (or already are) fixtures related to the Real Estate described in the mortgage
   - and (c) The mortgage complies with this section's requirements for a F/S (except that it need not state that it is to be filed in the Real Estate office)
   - and (d) The mortgage is duly recorded

ii) A fee for filing the F/S is not required; only the regular recording and satisfaction fees with respect to the mortgage are required.

(7) **Identity of the Debtor**

a) A F/S will be deemed to sufficiently show the identity of a Debtor if it gives the Individual, Partnership, or Corporate name of the Debtor (whether or not it adds other trade names or partners. Trade name alone is not adequate).

b) If Debtor changes its name, identity, or Corporate Structure (ex: merges) to the point that a filed F/S becomes *seriously misleading* then:

1. Perfection will be lost for all collateral acquired by the Debtor *more than* 4 Months *after* the change, *unless* 2. a new, appropriate F/S is filed within the 4 Months after the debtor changes his name/identity.

c) The F/S need not be change if a Debtor transfers the collateral (even if Secured Pty knows/consents to transfer) (Note: This does not apply to After-Acquired Property. A new F/S must be filed to perfect After-Acquired Property.)

(8) A F/S which contains *minor errors* is still valid if

a) It *substantially* complies with this subsection

and b) Errors are not *seriously misleading*

(must identify Creditor only enough to identify them or be able to contact them)

D. Where to File:

1. Interstate Place of Filing

OVERVIEW

- **Erroneous Filing**:
    - Erroneous Filings are not perfected, just *effective* regarding other perfected S/P's (§9-312)
    - Erroneous Filings, thus, are "ineffective" against Trustees in Bankruptcy
- Note: There is no need to file for motor vehicles and other items with Certificate of Title statutes.
- **Removal of Collateral**: 4 Month Rule - S/P has up to 4 Months to re-file in the appropriate office.

RELEVANT RULES: 9-401

§9-401: Place Of Filing (INTRASTATE):

(1) **Place of Filing:** The proper place, within a state, to file in order to perfect a S/I:

ALTERNATIVE I

(a) Office where Real Estate Mortgage would be filed for:

1. Natural Resources (oil, gas, minerals, timber)
2. Accounts subject to §9-103(5)
3. Fixture Financing Statement (as per §9-313) for goods which are (or will become) fixtures

(b) Office of the Secretary of State - for all other goods

ALTERNATIVE II

(a) In the County where Debtor lives (or where goods are kept if Debtor is not a resident of the state) for:

1) Farming Equipment or Products
2) General Intangibles arising/relating to the sale of farm products/equipment
3) Consumer goods
4) Growing Crops, or crops to be grown (must also file in county where land is located)

(b) Office where Real Estate Mortgage would be filed for:

1. Natural Resources (oil, gas, minerals, timber)
2. Accounts subject to §9-103(5)
3. Fixture Financing Statement (as per §9-313) for goods which are (or will become) fixtures

(c) Office of the Secretary of State - for all other goods

ALTERNATIVE III

(a) In the County where Debtor lives (or where goods are kept if Debtor is not a resident of the state) for:

1) Farming Equipment or Products
2) General Intangibles arising/relating to the sale of Farm Products/Equipment
3) Consumer Goods
4) Growing Crops - or crops to be grown (must also file in county where land is located)

(b) Office where Real Estate Mortgage would be filed for:

1) Natural Resources (oil, gas, minerals, timber)
2) Accounts subject to §9-103(5)
3) Fixture Financing Statement (as per §9-313) for goods which are (or will become) fixtures

(c) Office of the Secretary of State - for **all other goods,** *plus,* must also file:

1) In the county where the Debtor does business (if Debtor only does business in one county in the state)

or 2) In the County where Debtor resides (if Debtor resides in state but has no place of business in state)

(2) <u>**Erroneous Filing**</u> (within the correct State):

a) Erroneous Filings are still *effective* (but not perfected) with regard to:
1) Any of the collateral as to which the filing did comply with the filing requirements (of the UCC) (ex- if some of the collateral under the Security Agreement was properly filed, that collateral is protected (i.e. the entire Security Agreement is not ineffective))
and 2) Collateral covered by the Financing Statement against anyone who knew the contents of it

b) In order for an Erroneous Filing to be effective:
1) It must have been made in Good Faith and *either:*
a) Is filed in an improper place in the <u>proper state</u>
or b) Is not filed in <u>all</u> the required places
or 2) Future Secured Ptys have **Actual Knowledge** of erroneous filing (Note: Lien-holders and trustees in bankruptcy usually don't have knowledge, since they are not required to look at file)

(3) <u>**Removal of Collateral**</u>
Creditor need not re-file (to continue the effectiveness of the original filing) even if:
1. The use of the collateral changes
or 2. The collateral is moved (or either debtor's residence or place of business changes (whichever determined where to originally file)) .

ALTERNATIVE
a) Filing made in the proper county continues to be effective for up to <u>4 Months.</u> after Debtor/collateral has moved (change of use does not effect filing).
b) A Copy of the signed Financing Statement must be re-filed in the new county within the 4 Month period in order to continue effectiveness of filing (i.e. perfection).
c) The S/I may be "re-perfected" in the new county after the 4 Month period, in which case, <u>Perfection Date = Time of New Filing</u> (in the new county) (thus, you lose priority to any Lien Creditors who 'attach' in before the new filing).

(*** Note: Change of Use does not impair the effectiveness of the original filing.)

(4) <u>**Filing Requirement:**</u> §9-103 determines whether filing is necessary in the state.

(5) **Transmitting Utilities and Fixture Filing:**

a) The proper place for filing a Fixture or Transmitting Utility is the Secretary of State.

b) This section is Subject to §9-302(3)

c) This section supersedes any previous sections above (i.e. §9-401)

(6) **Residence** - (see also 9-103)

a) For purposes of this section, the Residence of an Organization is

1) It's place of business (if it has only one)

2) Where its Chief Executive Office is (if it has more than one place of business)

b) Use this subsection only if Alternatives II or III of §9-401(1) are used.

2. *MULTI-STATE TRANSACTIONS*

OVERVIEW

- The best thing for a Creditor to do is to file in any state where he thinks the Debtor will use/take collateral.

- <u>**Basic Rules**</u>
    - Goods, Documents, Instruments (ordinarily perfected by filing) - **Last Events Test** (see §9-103(1)(b))
    - Chattel Paper in possession - Last Events Test
    - Chattel Paper filed - Debtor's location
    - Accounts, Intangibles, Mobile Goods (<u>intended for lease</u>) - Debtor's Location
    - Certificate of Title (ex: Motor Vehicles) - see law of issuing State
    - Minerals - Law of state where minerals were mined
    - Uncertified Securities - law of state of issuing organization
- **Last Events Test:**
    - This test is used to determine if perfection occurred under the applicable state law.
    - Example: If goods are in Iowa when X claims a Judicial Lien, we look to see if the goods were ever perfected in Iowa (and is still valid under Iowa law)

- **Goods Intended for use in Another Jurisdiction**:
  - This exception only applies to PMSI's
  - After the <u>30-Day</u> period (specified in §9-103(1)(c)) expires, if Debtor still has not brought collateral into state, then the Last Event Test is used.
  - Note: 30 Days begin upon Delivery to the Debtor
  - It would be Smart for the S/P to deliver the goods directly to the "intended" state or to file in each state it is expected to pass through (before it arrives at its "intended" destination)

- **Four Month Rule**: Goods remain perfected <u>4 Months</u> after being taken out of state (§9-103(1)(d))
  - Continuity is lost if a Creditor fails to re-perfect its S/I within the 4 Month period
  - 4 Months are cut short if original filing expires before 4 Month period ends
  - No need to re-perfect if perfection occurred by Automatic perfection (since there was no need to file in the first place)

RELEVANT RULES: 9-103

<u>§9-103: Perfecting Multi-State Transactions:</u>

(1) **<u>Documents, Instruments, and Ordinary Goods:</u>** (i.e. Collateral must have a definite location)

(a) <u>This section does not apply to:</u>

1) Certificates of Title (as per §9-103(2))

or 2) Mobile Goods (as per §9-103(3))

or 3) Minerals (as per §9-103(5))

(b) **"Last Events Test":** Rules of Perfection are governed by the laws of the Jurisdiction where the **last** event that is claimed to perfect (or "unperfect") the collateral occurs (a.k.a. "ALL EVENTS TEST").

(c) **PMSI Exception:** If parties creating a PMSI **understand**, *at the time the S/I attaches*, that the goods will be kept in another jurisdiction (i.e. the "proposed jurisdiction"), then the law of the jurisdiction where goods are to be taken applies:

1) Proposed Jurisdiction's laws apply from the time attachment occurs.
2) If goods are actually taken to their proposed jurisdiction, those laws remain in effect.
3) If the goods do not end up in their proposed jurisdiction then the proposed jurisdiction's laws apply for 30 Days from the date of **possession by Debtor**.

(d) **Removal of Collateral:**

1) If collateral is removed from a state where it is subject to the laws of its jurisdiction, the S/I remains perfected.
2) If "Action" to perfect a S/I is required (ex: State requires this type of collateral to be filed), then:
   - (i) The S/I becomes Unperfected (against Purchasers of the collateral after removal) if the "Action" is not taken before the *earlier of:*
     - a) The Expiration period of the original jurisdiction's filing
     - or b) 4 Months after the collateral is brought into the new state
   - (ii) The S/I Continues to be Perfected if the "Action" is taken before the *earlier of:*
     - a) The expiration period of the original jurisdiction's filing
     - or b) 4 Months after the collateral is brought into the new state

(iii) Priority over a BIOC of Consumer Goods (as per §9-307(2)) for collateral which has been removed from its original jurisdiction, has the same "Action" requirements as above ((i), (ii)).

(2) **Certificate of Title**

(Note: This section only applies to goods subject to Certificate of Title statutes; Motor Vehicles generally are not subject to such statutes until they are sold to a purchaser; thus, a new motor vehicle in possession of a retail dealer will probably be subject to (1) or, if the Motor Vehicle is to be leased, subject to (3))

(a) This section applies to goods which require a Certificate of Title (on which a S/I is required to be indicated upon (in order to perfect)).

(b) The law of the jurisdiction **issuing the certificate** governs until:

1) The Certificate is Surrendered

or 2) The *Later of*:

a) 4 Months after removal of the goods from the original jurisdiction

or b) The goods are registered in another jurisdiction

(*** Note: After expiration of the above period, goods are not covered by the Certificate Title within the meaning of this section)

(c) Goods not subject to a Certificate of Title statute in their original jurisdiction are subject to §9-103(d) if they are moved to a jurisdiction requiring a Certificate of Title (unless bought by a Buyer - as discussed in (d) below)

(d) Exception to 4 Month Rule:

If Perfected goods are brought into a new state, and the new state issues a Certificate of Title, *not showing the S/I*, the S/I becomes **Subordinate** to the rights of a Buyer who:

1) Is not a "Merchant" - Isn't in the business of selling the goods

and 2) Gives value

and 3) Receives delivery

and 4) Is Without Knowledge of the S/I

(3) **Accounts, General Intangibles, and Mobile Goods** (Not inventory which isn't leased!):

(a) This section applies to the following if it is not subject to a Certificate of Title statute (as per §9-103(2)):

1) **Accounts** and **General Intangibles** other than uncertified securities

and 2) **Mobile Goods** - Mobile Goods have the following Characteristics:

a) Goods of the type which are normally used in more than one jurisdiction (ex: cars, airplanes)

and b) They are Mobile

and c) They are *either:*

1. **Equipment** - expected to be moved or which have no definite location.

or 2. **Inventory** - to be LEASED by the Debtor to others (see §9-109:Mobile Goods)

(b) The laws of the jurisdiction where the **Debtor is located** governs (laws of perfection, non-perfection, and its effects)

(c) Foreign jurisdiction:

1) The law of the jurisdiction of debtor's main executive office in the U.S. applies if:

a) The Debtor is located outside the USA

and b) The Foreign country does not provide for filing/recording for perfection

2) S/I may be perfected by notifying the Account Debtor if

a) The Debtor is located outside the USA or Canada

and b) The Collateral is Accounts or General Intangibles

(d) **Debtor's location:**

1) Place of business - under normal circumstances
2) Chief executive office -if more than one place of business
3) Residence -if no place of business
4) Location of designated agent for Service of Process - if a foreign air carrier

(e) **Debtor Changes Location**

1) Perfection made in the place of debtor's location lasts until the earlier of:
   a) 4 Months after Debtor moves
   or b) Expiration of the original filing - when perfection would have ceased by the law of the first jurisdiction
2) If perfection is not made in the new jurisdiction before the expiration of the above period, then the security becomes unperfected, and is deemed *unperfected* as to a Purchaser of the collateral (after the change of location).

(4) **Chattel Paper**

a) Possessory S/I - §9-103(1) *"Last Events Test"* applies if the Chattel Paper is in the possession of the S/P
b) Non-Possessory S/I - §9-103(3) applies (file in Debtor's location) if the Chattel Paper is not in the possession of the S/P
c) A S/I in Chattel Paper may not be perfected by notification to the Account Debtor.

(5) **Minerals**

The law of the jurisdiction where the **minerals came from** governs perfection when the mineral attaches *either:*

a) As it is exacted
or b) To an account resulting from the sale of the minerals (at the wellhead or minehead)

(6) **Investment Property**

(a) This subsection applies to <u>investment property</u>; it lists the choice of law rules for perfection of security interests in investment property:

(b) **<u>Certificated Security</u>:** During the time that a security certificate is located in a jurisdiction, the following are governed by *the local law of the jurisdiction where the certificate is located* (except as otherwise provided in paragraph (f)):

1. Perfection of a security interest in a certificated security

and 2. The effect of perfection or non-perfection of the security interest

and 3. The priority of the security interest

(c) **<u>Uncertificated Security</u>:** The following are governed by *the local law of the issuer's jurisdiction as specified in Section 8-110(d)* (except as otherwise provided in paragraph (f)):

1. Perfection of a security interest in an uncertificated security

and 2. The effect of perfection or non-perfection of the security interest

and 3. The priority of the security interest

(d) **<u>Security Entitlements/Securities Accounts</u>:** The following are governed by *the local law of the securities intermediary's jurisdiction as specified in Section 8-110(e)* (except as otherwise provided in paragraph (f)):

1. Perfection of a security interest in a security entitlement or securities account

and 2. The effect of perfection or non-perfection of the security interest

and 3. The priority of the security interest

(e) **Commodity Contracts/Commodity Accounts:**

a. The following are governed by *the local law of the commodity intermediary's jurisdiction* (except as otherwise provided in paragraph (f)):

1. Perfection of a security interest in a commodity contract or commodity account

and 2. The effect of perfection or non-perfection of the security interest

and 3. The priority of the security interest

b. The following rules determine what **"commodity intermediary's jurisdiction"** means for purposes of this paragraph:

(i) **Jurisdiction Specified in Agreement:** The "commodity intermediary's jurisdiction" will be the jurisdiction specified in an agreement, if the agreement between the commodity intermediary and commodity customer specifies that it is governed by the law of a particular jurisdiction.

(ii) **Office of Commodity Account Specified in Agreement:** The "commodity intermediary's jurisdiction" will be the jurisdiction specified in an agreement, if:

1. The agreement between the commodity intermediary and commodity customer does not specify the governing law as provided in subparagraph (i).

but 2. It expressly specifies that the commodity account is maintained at an office in a particular jurisdiction.

(iii) **Location Not Specified in Agreement:** The "commodity intermediary's jurisdiction" will be the jurisdiction in which the office identified (in an account statement) as the office serving the commodity customer's account is located, if the agreement between the commodity intermediary and commodity customer does not specify a jurisdiction as provided in subparagraphs (i) or (ii).

(iv) **Location Not Specified and Office Not Identified:** The "commodity intermediary's jurisdiction" will be the jurisdiction in which the chief executive office of the commodity intermediary is located, if:

1. The agreement between the commodity intermediary and commodity customer does not specify a jurisdiction as provided in subparagraphs (i) or (ii).

and 2. An account statement does not identify an office serving the commodity customer's account as provided in subparagraph (iii).

(f) The following are governed by *the local law of the jurisdiction in which the debtor is located:*

1. Perfection of a security interest by filing
2. Automatic perfection of a security interest in **investment property** granted by a broker or securities intermediary
3. Automatic perfection of a security interest in a **commodity contract** or **commodity account** granted by a commodity intermediary

3. *Removal Of Collateral:* 4 Month Rule

OVERVIEW

- **Inter-State removal:** When collateral is moved to a new state the S/P must re-file the F/S within 4 Months after the collateral has entered the new state (See §9-103(1)(d)) (ex: Collateral left New York on January 1, and remained in New Jersey until March 1. Thereafter was moved to California. It arrived in California on April 1, and stayed there permanently. The S/P does not have to file in New Jersey. He must only file in California, within 4 Months after it arrived, i.e. the S/P must file before August 1.)

- Intra-State removal: If collateral is moved to a different county (or filing jurisdiction) in the *same state*, the S/P does not always have to re-file. The S/P will only have to re-file if the state (in which the collateral is in) has adopted the alternative to §9-401(3).

- Goods remain perfected 4 Months after Removal (out of state: §9-103(1)d); within state: §9-401(3)), but:
  - Continuity is lost if you fail to re-perfect within 4 Month period

  and
  - The 4 Month grace period will be cut short if original filing expires before 4 Month period ends.

  and
  - There is a need to re-perfect if perfection occurred by Automatic perfection (since there was no need to file in the first place)

RELEVANT RULES: 9-103(1)(d), (3)

§9-103(1)(d): Removal of Collateral to Another State:

1) Collateral must be **Documents, Instruments, and Ordinary Goods:** (i.e.- collateral must have a definite location)

2) If collateral is removed from a state where it is subject to the laws of its jurisdiction, the S/I remains perfected.

3) If "Action" to perfect a S/I is required (ex: State requires this type of collateral to be filed), then:

- (i) The S/I becomes Unperfected (against Purchasers of the collateral after removal) if the "Action" is not taken before the *earlier of:*
  - a) The Expiration period of the original jurisdiction's filing
  - or b) 4 Months after the collateral is brought into the new state
- (ii) The S/I Continues to be Perfected if the "Action" is taken before the *earlier of:*
  - a) The expiration period of the original jurisdiction's filing
  - or b) 4 Months after the collateral is brought into the new state
- (iii) Priority over a BIOC of Consumer Goods (as per §9-307(2)) for collateral which has been removed from its original jurisdiction, has the same "Action" requirements as above ((i), (ii)).

§9-401(3) Removal of Collateral within the Same State:

(3) **Removal of Collateral**

Creditor need not re-file (to continue the effectiveness of the original filing) even if:

1. The use of the collateral changes

or 2. The collateral is moved (or either debtor's residence or place of business changes (whichever determined where to originally file)) .

ALTERNATIVE

a) Filing made in the proper county continues to be effective for up to 4 Months. after Debtor/collateral has moved (change of use does not effect filing).

b) A Copy of the signed Financing Statement must be re-filed in the new county within the 4 Month period in order to continue effectiveness of filing (i.e. perfection).

c) The S/I may be "re-perfected" in the new county after the 4 Month period, in which case, Perfection Date = Time of New Filing (in the new county) (thus, you lose priority to any Lien Creditors who 'attach' in before the new filing).

(*** Note: Change of Use does not impair the effectiveness of the original filing.)

4. *AUTOMATIC PERFECTION (See §9-302)*

OVERVIEW

- Attachment is the only requirement in Automatic Perfection
- The following can be Automatically Perfected:
    - **Beneficial Interests** (§9-302(1)(c))
    - **Assignment of Accounts** - only if they do not constitute a *significant portion* of the Assignor's outstanding debts to *that Assignee* (§9-302(1)(e))
    - **After-Acquired Property** - already covered by original, Perfected S/A (w/ a filing) (§9-204(1))
    - **PMSI in Consumer Goods** - no filing required
        - A PMSI may be secured by anyone giving value for purchase (ex: seller or bank)
        - Money must be Actually Used for the purchase of Consumer Goods
        - Unlike regular perfection, the S/I is only in the money given for purchase (initial money given; Future Advances are, thus, subject to intermediate liens)
        - Security Agreement must be specific and signed by Debtor
        - S/P must believe goods are to be used as Consumer Goods
        - Note: Motor Vehicles are *specifically excluded* from Consumer Goods (see §9-302(1)(d))

- Automatic **Re-Perfection in Proceeds**: This will occur in 2 situations:
  - When the proceeds are Non-cash proceeds -if they are of a type of collateral which may be perfected by filing in the office where the original F/S is located.

  and
  - When the proceeds are Non-cash proceeds, which were obtained from Cash-proceeds of the original collateral - if they are of a type of collateral covered by the description in the original F/S.

- **Investment Property** - Investment Property can be automatically perfected as with **Control**, and no Security Agreement is needed (§9-115; §9-116)

RELEVANT RULES: 9-302(1)(c), (d), (e); 9-109(1); 9-306(3)(a); 9-204(1)

§9-302(1)(c)-(e): Filing Not Required

* * *

or (c) A S/I created by an Assignment of a Beneficial Interest in a Trust (or a decedents estate)

or (d) **A PMSI in CONSUMER GOODS,** unless it is for

1. Motor Vehicles required to be registered

or 2. Fixtures (as per §9-313)

or (e) An **Assignment of Accounts,** which does not transfer a significant part of the assignor's accounts (alone or in conjunction with other assignments to the same Assignee)

§9-109(1): Consumer Goods:

"Consumer Goods" - goods used or bought primarily for personal, family, or household purposes.

§9-306(3)(a),(c): Automatic Re-perfection in Proceeds

(a) **AUTOMATIC RE-PERFECTION** occurs; Automatic re-perfection occurs if *either:*

1. Non-Cash Proceeds: (ex: a car for a car)
    a. The *filed* Financing Statement covers the original collateral
    and b. The proceeds are collateral in which a S/I may be perfected by filing (i.e. not cash) in the office where the Financing Statement was filed (even if you don't re-file) (Default Rule: silence means you have a S/I in proceeds)

or 2. Non-Cash Proceeds bought with Cash Proceeds: If the *non-cash proceeds on* are acquired with ***cash- proceeds***, perfection continues if the Financing Statement indicates the types of property constituting the proceeds (ex: a car for cash, to buy a new car).

or (b) Proceeds are **CASH PROCEEDS** (ex: Accounts), AND:
1. Cash-proceeds are identifiable
and 2. A *filed* Financing Statement covers the original collateral

or (c) The S/I in the proceeds is perfected before the *10 Day* period expires.

§9-204(1): Automatic Perfection in After-Acquired Property

A S/A may provide for After-Acquired Property to secure the obligations covered by the S/A (except as provided below in (2)).

5. *TEMPORARY AUTOMATIC PERFECTION*

OVERVIEW

- Temporary Automatic Perfection Occurs in:
    - **PMSI's** - for 10 Days (§9-301(2))
    - **Proceeds** not automatically perfected- for 10 Days (§9-306(3)(c))
    - **Instruments** - for 21 Days (§9-304(4), (5))
    - Certain **Negotiable Documents** - for 21 Days (§9-304(4), (5))
    - **Certificated Securities** - for 21 Days (§9-304(4), (5))

RELEVANT RULES: 9-302(1)(b); 9-306(3); 9-304(4), (5)

§9-302(1)(b): Filing Is Not Required

A S/I **temporarily perfected,** *either:*

1. In instruments or documents, without delivery (as per §9-304 - 21 Day rule)

or 2. In proceeds for a 10 Day period (as per §9-306)

§9-306(3): Temporary Perfection in Proceeds:

The Security Interest in Proceeds

i) A S/I in Proceeds is considered *Continuously Perfected* if the original collateral was "re-perfected" within 10 Days (of "conversion" to proceeds) (i.e. the date of perfection in the Proceeds relates back to date the original collateral was perfected).

ii) The Proceeds becomes unperfected 10 Days after the Debtor receives the proceeds - Unless they are "re-perfected" (within the 10 day period).

iii) A S/I in proceeds can only be perfected by the rules spelled out in the UCC, for *original collateral of the same type*.

iv) Perfection can be continuously maintained in Proceeds if:

(a) **AUTOMATIC RE-PERFECTION** occurs; Automatic re-perfection occurs if *either:*

1. Non-Cash Proceeds: (ex: a car for a car)
   a. The *filed* Financing Statement covers the original collateral

   and b. The proceeds are collateral in which a S/I may be perfected by filing (i.e. not cash) in the office where the Financing Statement was filed (even if you don't re-file) (Default Rule: silence means you have a S/I in proceeds)

or 2. Non-Cash Proceeds bought with Cash Proceeds: If the *non-cash proceeds on* are acquired with ***cash-proceeds***, perfection continues if the Financing Statement indicates the types of property constituting the proceeds (ex: a car for cash, to buy a new car).

or (b) Proceeds are **CASH PROCEEDS** (ex: Accounts), AND:
1. Cash-proceeds are identifiable

and 2. A *filed* Financing Statement covers the original collateral

or (c) The orginal collateral was Investment Property and the proceeds are Identifiable Cash proceeeds

or (d) The S/I in the proceeds is perfected before the *10 Day* period expires.

§9-304(4),(5): Temporary Perfection Of Instruments:

(4) Temporary Perfection Without Filing

a) A S/I is automatically perfected for 21 Days from the time of **attachment** (even without proper filing or possession) for:

1) Instruments

and 2) Negotiable Documents (only includes goods in a Bailee's possession if it made a Negotiable Document for those goods)

and 3) Certificated Securities

b) Requirements for Automatic Temporary perfection:

1) The S/I must arise under a *written* Security Agreement

and 2) *New value* must be given for the S/I

(5) Continued Perfection when Collateral is Given to Debtor

A S/I remains perfected for 21 Days (without filing) if

1) A Secured Pty has a Perfected S/I in:

a) An Instrument

or b) A Negotiable Document

or c) Goods in the possession of a Bailee

or d) A Certificated Security

and 2) The S/P has:

(a) Made available Goods or Documents to the Debtor for the purpose of:

1) Ultimate Sale or Exchange

or 2) Loading/Unloading/Storing

or 3) Shipping/Transshipping

or 4) Manufacturing/Processing

or 5) Dealing with them in a manner preliminary to sale/exchange

**** Note: Priority between conflicting S/I's in goods are subject to §9-312(3)

or (b) Delivered Instruments or Certificated Securities to the Debtor for the purpose of:

1) Ultimate sale or exchange

or 2) Presentation (for sale)

or 3) Collection

or 4) Renewal

or 5) Registration of Transfer

(6) After the 21 Day Period, the S/I must be perfected by complying with the applicable provisions in Article 9 if:

a) It is still not perfected (as per (4))

or b) It is still in debtor's possession (as per (5))

IV. PRIORITIES

1. PRIORITIES IN SECURITY INTERESTS

OVERVIEW

- "Lien Creditor" refers to a:
    - Judicial Lien Creditor - with a lien obtained from a court (ex: tort claim lien)
    - or Trustee in Bankruptcy - with a lien obtained through its "avoidance powers" (see Bankruptcy section)
    - or Statutory Lienholder - with an automatic lien created by statute (ex: tax lien)
- Time that a Lien Creditor's interest takes effect:
    - Judicial - at the time of levy
    - Trustee - upon filing of Bankruptcy petition
    - Statutory - as specified in statute

RELEVANT RULES: 9-301; 9-310

§9-301: Priority Over Unperfected Security Interests:

(1) Classes of People who take Priority over an Unperfected Security Interest

(a) A **Perfected S/P** entitled to priority under §9-312

or (b) A person who becomes a **Lien Creditor** *before* the Security Interest is Perfected (but see (2))

or (c) **A Buyer:** Requirements to qualify as a "Buyer":

1) The Buyer must be *either:*

a) A Buyer not in the Ordinary Course of Business

or b) A Bulk Transferee

or c) A Buyer of Farm Products - in the Ordinary Course of Business

and 2) The Buyer cannot be a Secured Pty

and 3) The Buyer must:

a) Have *No Knowledge* of the S/I

and b) Give *Value*

and c) *Receive delivery* (of collateral) before the S/I is perfected

and 4) The Collateral must either be:

a) Goods

or b) Instruments

or c) Documents

or d) Chattel Paper

or (d) **Transferee of Accounts, General Intangibles, or Certified Securities** who:

1) Gives value before they are perfected

and 2) Is without knowledge of S/I

and 3) Is not a Secured Pty

(2) **PMSI Exception:** A Secured Pty takes priority over any Lien Creditor or "Bulk Transferee" (whose rights arise between the time of attachment and filing) if the Secured Pty files a PMSI:

a) Before Debtor receives the collateral (i.e. before attachment)

or b) Within 10 Days after Debtor receives **Possession** of the collateral

(3) A **Lien Creditor** is

a) A Creditor who obtains a Lien on property involved *by attachment, levy,* or the like

or b) An Assignee for the Benefit of Creditors from the time of assignment

or c) A Trustee in Bankruptcy from the date of the filing of the petition

or d) A Receiver in Equity from the time of appointment

(4) A person who becomes a Lien Creditor after a S/I is perfected, takes subject to that S/I only if it:

a) Secures **Future Advances** made to Debtor:

1. Before the Third Pty becomes a Lien Creditor

or 2. Within 45 Days *after* the Third Pty becomes a Lien Creditor

or b) Is made **Without Knowledge** of the Lien

or c) Is made pursuant to a **Prior Commitment** entered into *without knowledge* of the lien

§9-310: Priority Of Certain Liens Arising By Operation Of Law:

1) A person will have a Lien on goods if:

a) She furnishes services or materials for the secured goods

and b) It is done in the Ordinary Course of his business

and c) she retains Possession of the goods

and d) There is a Statute or Rule of law creating a lien for such services or materials

2) This Possessory, Statutory Lien will take Priority over a Perfected S/I *unless:*

a) The lien arises only by Statute

and b) The Statute expressly provides otherwise

2. *CONFLICTING SECURITY INTERESTS*

OVERVIEW

- §9-301 applies to all creditors; §9-312 only governs priorities between secured parties.

- General Rule - **First to File** or **Perfect**: Priority is given to the person who either Files first OR Perfects first (ex: One may file before perfecting and maintain priority over someone who perfected before one perfected but after one filed.)

- **PMSI Super Priority** (9-312(4)): The reason for giving "Purchase Money" Secured Creditors "super priority," is because they are enabling the Debtor to obtain more property. This may not only put the Debtor in a better financial position, but it also does not reduce the S/P's interest. The rationale behind this is that since the Debtor could not have purchased the extra collateral without the "Purchase Money" Secured Party, another S/P, with an interest in After-Acquired property, would not have had the new PMSI collateral, *but for* the new creditor. Thus, the S/P is no worse off than he would have been without the Purchase Money Secured Party's "super-priority." In fact, the original S/P may be better off, especially if the "Purchase Money" Secured Pty has under-secured the new collateral.

- **§9-316** - Parties can stipulate Priority on their own.

RELEVANT RULES: 9-312; 9-316

§9-312: Priorities Among Conflicting Security Interests In The Same Collateral:

(Between Perfected S/P's only; for other priority conflicts see §9-301)

(1) **Scope:** Rules stated in other sections of Part 3, as well as the following other sections of the UCC shall govern when applicable:

a) §4-208 (S/I of Collecting Banks in items being collected, accompanying documents, and proceeds)

b) §9-103 (S/I related to other jurisdictions)

c) §9-114 (Consignments)

d) §9-115 (S/I in Investment Property)

(2) **S/I in Crops**:

a) A Perfected S/I in crops takes priority over an earlier perfected S/I if:

1. The New Creditor gave value to enable Debtor to produce the crops during the production season

and 2. The New Creditor gave money within 3 Mos. before the crops become "growing crops" (ex: by planting them)

and 3. The Earlier S/I secures obligations due more than 6 Months before crops became "growing crops"

b) It is irrelevant that New Creditor had knowledge of earlier S/I.

(3) **PMSI Super-Priority in INVENTORY:**

i) A Perfected PMSI in inventory has Priority over a conflicting S/I in the same inventory.

ii) PMSI "Super-Priority" applies Only to:

a) The same inventory

and b) Identifiable **cash proceeds** received on or before the day that Debtor delivers the inventory to a Third Pty buyer (OK if proceeds are money, checks, deposit accounts; No good if converted to cash proceeds; must be direct cash proceeds (ex: car-trade-ins are not good, Accounts receivable and Chattel Paper are also no good))

iii) Requirements for PMSI Priority

(a) The PMSI is perfected when Debtor receives possession of inventory.

and (b) The "Purchase Money" Secured Pty *gives written notice* to the conflicting Secured Pty only if the conflicting Secured Pty filed a financing statement covering the same types of inventory *before:*

(i) The "Purchase Money" Secured Pty filed (or Debtor receives Possession)

or (ii) The beginning of the 21 Day period (in which a PMSI is temporarily perfected without filing or possession (as per §9-304(5)))

and (c) The Conflicting Secured Pty received the notification within 5 Yrs before the Debtor receives possession of the inventory (i.e. since a notice is effective for 5 Yrs, S/P can continue making PMSI's without further notices within 5 yr. period)

and (d) The notice states that the person sending it expects to obtain a PMSI in the debtor's Inventory (describing the inventory by or type)

(4) **A PMSI in Non-Inventory Collateral** (ex: Equipment):

A Purchase-Money-Secured Pty has priority over conflicting secured parties in collateral or its proceeds if the:

a. PMSI is perfected at the time Debtor receives possession of the collateral

or b. PMSI is perfected within 10 Days after Debtor receives possession of collateral

(5) **First in Time, First in Right**: In all other cases (not specified above), priority between conflicting S/I's in the same collateral shall be determined according to the following rules:

(a) **First to Perfect:**

1. Conflicting S/I's Rank according to priority in Time of Filing or Perfection.
2. Priority dates back from the *earlier* of the first Perfection **or** Filing as long as later there is no period in which there is neither filing nor perfection (i.e. it is continuous).

(b) **The First to Attach** the collateral, if all conflicting S/I's are unperfected.

(6) The date of Filing/Perfection for collateral is the same date to apply to Proceeds of that collateral (for purposes for §9-312(5)).

(7) **Future Advances:**

a) A S/P will maintain the SAME PRIORITY (under (5) above or §9-115(5)) in *Future Advances* (as per §9-301(4)) as he did in his *original advance* (loan) if the Future Advances are made:

1) **After** the original S/I is perfected (by filing or possession (or under §9-115 or §9-116 on Investment property))

or 2) **Before/while** the S/I is perfected

b) In all other cases, a perfected S/I has priority from the date the advance was made (i.e. if you perfect collateral worth $10M and initial lien is for $2M (covering a $2M cash advancement), a subsequent advance for $6M will have the same priority as the first loan's lien).

§9-316: Priority Agreements:

Parties may agree to subordinate their priorities to other parties.

3. *PRIORITY OVER FUTURE ADVANCES*

OVERVIEW

- A Secured Party may obtain the same priority in collateral for value give at the time of the S/A and any "Future Advances." (ex: If A perfects a S/I in a car for $5,000 on Day 1 and B perfects a S/I in the car for $8,000 on Day 5, A maintains Priority; even if A advances another $6,000 on Day 8 – after B perfected -- A is entitled to $11,000 before B can collect his $8,000).

- **Future Advances** must be specified in a S/A in order for them to be secured.

- If the language of the S/A is too broad (i.e. "I grant you a S/I in this collateral for this loan and: "*All other Future Advances and Other Debt Obligations*") some courts will void the Future Advance provision entirely.

- Limitations: The following will take free of any Future Advances made 45 Days after the purchase (unless the Future Advances were pursuant to a prior commitment):
    - **Purchasers** - Non-BIOCs (see §9-307(3))
    - and **Lien Creditors** (see §9-301(4))

RELEVANT RULES: 9-204(3), 9-312(7); 9-301(4); 9-307(3)

§9-204(3): Future Advances:

a) Obligations covered by a S/A may include Future Advances or other value.
b) It is not necessary for the Future Advances to be given pursuant to a commitment (see 9-105(1)).

§9-312(7): Priority in Future Advances

a) A S/P will maintain the SAME PRIORITY (under (5) above or §9-115(5)) in *Future Advances* (as per §9-301(4)) as he did in his *original advance* (loan) if the Future Advances are made:
1) **After** the original S/I is perfected (by filing or possession (or under §9-115 and §8-321 for securities))
or 2) **Before/while** the S/I is perfected

b) In all other cases, a perfected S/I has priority from the date the advance was made (i.e. if you perfect collateral worth $10M and initial lien is for $2M (covering a $2M cash advancement), a subsequent advance for $6M will have the same priority as the first loan's lien).

§9-301(4): Priority Over Unperfected Security Interests:

(4) A person who becomes a Lien Creditor after a S/I is perfected, takes subject to that S/I only if it:
a) Secures **Future Advances** made to Debtor:
1. Before the Third Pty becomes a Lien Creditor
or 2. Within 45 Days *after* the Third Pty becomes a Lien Creditor
or b) Is made **Without Knowledge** of the Lien
or c) Is made pursuant to a **Prior Commitment** entered into *without knowledge* of the lien

§9-307(3): Protection Of Buyers Of Goods:

OTHER BUYERS: (Not Ordinary Course of Business):

a) A Buyer takes free of Future Advances covered by a S/I only if the Future Advances are made *before* the *earlier* of:

1. The time that the S/P acquires knowledge of the purchases

or 2. 45 Days after the purchase

b) A Buyer will NOT take free of Future Advances if they are made Pursuant to a Commitment entered into:

1. Without knowledge of the purchase

and 2. Before the expiration of the 45 day period

4. *PROCEEDS*

OVERVIEW

- Debtor's Right to Transfer Interest in Collateral
    - Debtor's have a right to dispose or sell the collateral or transfer their interests in it (see §9-311)
    - If the S/A prohibits such a transfer, the S/P may sue for Breach of Contract if the Debtor makes such a transfer; yet the transfer will still be effective (§9-311).
- In order to be considered proceeds, the remaining collateral must be classified under a §9-306(1) category
- No need to specify in the S/A that a S/I will cover proceeds (it is already assumed).
- The 10 Day "grace period" to re-file applies to proceeds which *cannot be perfected by a F/S already on file*; examples include:
    - Proceeds that may only be perfected by possession
    - Proceeds not covered by the description in the filed F/S
    - Original Collateral that was filed in a place other than where proceeds of that type are normally filed
    - Original Collateral that was perfected without filing (and the proceeds are not subject to automatic perfection (see AUTOMATIC PERFECTION above))
- Perfection can be maintained in the original collateral (unless bought by a Buyer In Due Course); The S/P may assert his interest in either the proceeds or the original collateral (which is in the hands of a Third Pty purchaser) (although S/P may claim BOTH proceeds and the original collateral, he may only obtain 1 satisfaction).

- **Conflicting Interests**
  - When Proceeds of Inventory becomes A/R, and another party already has a S/I in A/R, then whoever is First to File or Perfect their interest will take priority (see §9-312(5) above).
  - PMSI Priority - If a S/I in Inventory was a PMSI, §9-312(3)'s super-priority gives the "Purchase Money" Secured Pty priority in the Cash Proceeds (non-cash proceeds will be subject to "first-to-file or perfect" rule), ONLY IF the **Cash** proceeds were received on or before Debtor delivers inventory to Third Pty buyer (i.e. to qualify, purchases must be made COD or Pre-paid by purchaser; Purchases made on credit are <u>not included</u> in this exception)
- <u>**Special Cases**</u>:
  - **Insurance** made out to a Third Pty does not qualify as proceeds.
    - But it can be endorsed to make it an acceptable proceed.
    - Problem: During the time period between receiving Insurance check and when equipment is broken the claim will probably be considered to be a General Intangible (and one may have to file a F/S on the Insurance claims).
- **A/R:** For A/R to qualify as proceeds, it must
  - Show the source of Income (i.e. that it's proceeds from collateral)
  - and Either be:
    - Identifiable - not commingled
    - or Commingled - but received within <u>10 Days</u> of filing

- **Equipment**: Problems arise when proceeds are Equipment:
  - Unlike Inventory or A/R, equipment is not expected to be sold or exchanged (Inventory and A/R represent an inherent right in proceeds)
  - *Questions which often arise:* Do proceeds include work done with Equipment? Does it matter if Equipment depreciates with use?

  Note: There is a Problem because Equipment usually is used as part of a service, and people pay more for the service than for just the use of the Equipment (ex: building a house w/ a chain saw (which is collateral to a S/P's S/I); is the money from the building contract considered proceeds from saw?)
- **Tort Claims** - from collateral (i.e. if it breaks) is usually NOT considered proceeds, Unless it is a result of a Breach of Warranty
- **Leasing of Collateral** (by Debtor): usually considered proceeds (because it is considered to be a "Disposition")
- **<u>Cash Proceeds</u>**:
  - For purposes of §9-306(4)(d)(II), Cash is received by Debtor when he <u>Acquires Rights</u> in the cash (not necessarily possession)
  - Cash Dividends and Bond Payments are considered Cash Proceeds of securities
  - <u>Problem</u>: Since Cash is normally deposited into Deposit Accounts, problems arise when other cash is deposited; It becomes difficult to identify which "dollars" represent the proceeds to your collateral.

- Methods of Tracing:
  - "*Heavy Money Rule*" is the most commonly used method of tracing money. We use the LIBR (Lowest Intermediate Balance Rule); (i.e. Deduct [proceeds of any collateral covered in S/A] from [all expenses paid from the account] not adding [income from other sources]; Note: expenses get deducted first from proceeds, and then from other deposits)
  - Other methods give all proceeds received 10 Days before Bankruptcy petition is filed.

RELEVANT RULES: 9-306

§9-306: Rights In "Proceeds":

(1) **"Proceeds"**

a) Proceeds may be obtained from:

1. Whatever is received upon:
   a. Sale
   or b. Exchange
   or c. Collection
   or d. Other disposition (of collateral or proceeds)

or 2. Insurance payable from the loss/damage of the collateral, *unless* the insurance check is made payable to a non-party of the security agreement (Note: can be endorsed by Third Pty to become valid)

or 3. Any payments or distributions made with respect to investment property collateral.

b) Proceeds may be in the form of:

1. **Cash Proceeds** - Money, checks, deposit accounts, etc.
or 2. **Non-Cash Proceeds** - all other proceeds

(2) **Continuation of the S/I:** Unless otherwise provided by the UCC, a S/I in collateral continues in:

a) Collateral - even if it is sold/disposed of, unless the disposition was *authorized* by the Secured Pty
and b) Proceeds - ONLY if the proceeds are IDENTIFIABLE

(3) **The Security Interest in Proceeds**

i) A S/I in Proceeds is considered *Continuously Perfected* if the original collateral was "re-perfected" within 10 Days (of "conversion" to proceeds) (i.e. the date of perfection in the Proceeds relates back to date the original collateral was perfected).

ii) The Proceeds becomes unperfected 10 Days after the Debtor receives the proceeds - Unless they are "re-perfected" (within the 10 day period).

iii) A S/I in proceeds can only be perfected by the rules spelled out in the UCC, for *original collateral of the same type*.

iv) Perfection can be continuously maintained in Proceeds if:

(a) **AUTOMATIC RE-PERFECTION** occurs; Automatic re-perfection occurs if *either:*

1. Non-Cash Proceeds: (ex: a car for a car)

a. The *filed* Financing Statement covers the original collateral

and b The proceeds are collateral in which a S/I may be perfected by filing (i.e. not cash) in the office where the Financing Statement was filed (even if you don't re-file) (Default Rule: silence means you have a S/I in proceeds)

or 2. Non-Cash Proceeds bought with Cash Proceeds: If the *non-cash proceeds on* are acquired with ***cash- proceeds***, perfection continues if the Financing Statement indicates the types of property constituting the proceeds (ex: a car for cash, to buy a new car).

or (b) Proceeds are **CASH PROCEEDS** (ex: Accounts), AND:

1. Cash-proceeds are identifiable

and 2. A *filed* Financing Statement covers the original collateral

or (c) The orginal collateral was Investment Property and the proceeds are Identifiable Cash proceeeds

or (d) The S/I in the proceeds is perfected before the *10 Day* period expires.

(4) S/I in proceeds of an Insolvent Debtor - A S/P (with a perfected S/I in proceeds) can only maintain a S/I in:

(a) **Non-Cash Proceeds**, which are
1. Identifiable
and 2. In a separate deposit account, containing only proceeds

or (b) **Money Cash-Proceeds**, which are
1. Identifiable
and 2. In the form of money
and 3. Not commingled with other money
and 4. Not deposited into a deposit account *prior* to insolvency

or (c) **Instrument Cash-Proceeds** (i.e. checks, notes), which are
1. Identifiable
and 2. Not deposited in a deposit account *prior* to insolvency proceedings

or (d) **Cash-Proceeds in Accounts -** In all cash and deposit accounts of the Debtor (in which proceeds have been commingled) perfection may be maintained, yet it will be:
(i) Subject to any right to set-off
and (ii) Limited to:
An "Amount" ($\leq$ any cash-proceeds received by Debtor within 10 days of insolvency)
less - (I) Payments to S/P on "account of cash proceeds" (within 10 Day period)
less - (II) Cash Proceeds received by Debtor during 10 Day period

(5) Priorities with Returned/Repossessed Goods

i) **Requirements for Priority:**

a) The Sale of goods must result in an Account or Chattel Paper which is transferred by the seller to the S/P.

and b) The goods must be *returned* or *repossessed* by the Debtor or the S/P.

ii) **Rules of Priorities for Returned/Repossessed Goods**

(a) RE-PERFECTION: The Original Security Interest *re-attaches* to the goods, continuing perfection if:

1. The goods were collateral at the time of the sale

and 2. The debt attached to collateral not paid at the sale

and 3. It was perfected when the goods were sold

and 4. *Either:*

a. If **Perfection by Filing:** S/P files a new F/S *only* if the original Filing is not still effective

or b. If **Non-Filed Perfection:** S/P takes possession of goods or file a new F/S

(b) CHATTEL PAPER:

1. An unpaid Transferee of the Chattel Paper maintains a S/I in the goods against the transferor.

2. If Transferee of Chattel Paper is entitled to priority (pursuant to §9-308), then he takes priority over RE-PERFECTED Secured Ptys (see (a)above).

(c) ACCOUNTS:

1. An unpaid Transferee of an account has a S/I in goods against the Transferor.

2. This S/I is *subordinate* to a re-perfected S/I (see (a) above)

(d) A S/I of an unpaid transferee (pursuant to (b) and (c)) must be perfected to protect themselves against

1. Creditors of the Transferor

and 2. Purchasers of the returned/repossessed goods

5. *ACCESSIONS AND PROCESSED GOODS*

RELEVANT RULES: 9-314; 9-315

§9-314: Accessions:

(1) **Security Interest Attached Before Installation**

a. A S/P with an interest in goods ("input goods") which attach *before* they become installed or affixed to other goods retains priority over those input goods, against claims over the "whole" (i.e. the goods which they are attached to).

b. In order to maintain priority, the S/I must *attach* to the goods before they are installed or affixed to other goods (i.e. the "whole").

c. The S/I in the original, input goods takes *priority* over any party's claim in the Whole (i.e. the final product), subject to:

a) §9-315(1) (Commingled Goods)

b) §9-314(3) (Exceptions)

(2) **Security Interest Attached After Installation**

a. A S/I attached to Accessions (i.e. the original, input goods) *after* they become part of a Whole is **valid** against any subsequent S/I's in the Whole (subject to the exceptions in (3) below).

b. The S/I is **invalid** against anyone with a S/I in the Whole *before* the S/I attaches to the Accessions, *unless* the S/P with an interest in the Whole *either:*

1. **Consents** *in writing* to the S/I in the Accessions

or 2. **Disclaims** *in writing* its interest in the Accessions as part of the whole.

(3) **Exceptions**: The S/I's described above in (1) and (2) do not take priority over:

(a) A "*Subsequent Purchaser,*" if he buys:

1. Any interest in the Whole for **value**

and 2. **Without Knowledge** of the S/I

and 3. ***Before*** the S/I in the Accessions is perfected

(**** Note: A Purchaser of the Whole at a foreclosure sale is considered to be a "Subsequent Purchaser" within this section (unless the purchaser is the holder of a perfected S/I, buying at his own foreclosure sale))

(b) A Judicial Lien Creditor, if:
1. A Lien on the Whole is *subsequently* obtained by judicial proceedings
and 2. The Lien is obtained **Without Knowledge** of the S/I
and 3. The Lien is obtained *before* the S/I in the Accessions is perfected

(c) Future Advances if:
1. Creditor making Future Advances has a Prior Perfected S/I in the Whole
and 2. Creditor *contracts for* or *makes* Future Advances **Without Knowledge** of the S/I
and 3. Creditor *contracts for* or *makes* Future Advance *before* the S/I in the input goods is Perfected.

(4) **Removal of Collateral Upon Default**

a. If a S/P's interest in the accessions has priority over *all* other Secured Parties with interests in the Whole (pursuant to (1), (2), and (3) above), he may remove his collateral from the Whole if the Debtor defaults (subject to Part 5).

b. The S/P must reimburse any Encumbrancer or Owner of the Whole for the cost to repair any *physical injury* resulting from the removal of the collateral if:
1 The Owner or Encumbrancer is not the Debtor
or 2. The Owner or Encumbrancer has not otherwise agreed

c. The S/P need NOT Reimburse the Owner or Encumbrancer for
1. Any loss in value of the Whole caused by the absence of the removed goods
or 2. The loss incurred by any necessity of *replacing* the goods

d. Those entitled to reimbursement may *refuse* permission for the S/P to remove his collateral until he gives them *adequate security* that he will reimburse them for the appropriate damages.

§9-315: Priority When Goods Which Are Commingled Or Processed:

(1) If a S/I in goods is perfected, and those goods are *later* used as inputs for end products, the S/I continues in those end products if:

(a) The identity of the goods are lost - in the end product

or (b) A Financing Statement covering the *Original Goods* also covers the end product (which the input goods have been placed into)

(Note: A separate S/I in the inputs (as per §9-314) may not be taken in addition to the S/I in the end products (i.e. choice of one or the other))

(2) If there are different S/I's in the different goods which form the end product (ex: X has a $100 perfected S/I in cotton and Y has a $200 perfected S/I in the polyester. The debtor converts this into $600 worth of shirts. X has an interest of 1/6 and Y has an interests of 2/6), then the S/I's rank **Equally** according to the Ratio of:

$$\frac{\textbf{Cost of Original Goods}}{\textbf{Cost of End Product}}$$

V. EXCEPTIONS TO NORMAL PRIORITY RULES

A. BUYERS IN THE ORDINARY COURSE

OVERVIEW

- Any Buyer takes free of unperfected S/I's
- Perfected S/I's continues in collateral even though it is purchased.
- The S/P may claim the Proceeds or the sold Collateral (if it is not sold to a BIOC) (see §9-306(2)).
- BIOCs can take free of a *Perfected* S/I only if the collateral was *Inventory*
- A Perfected S/I sold to a Non-BIOC may become unperfected, however, if the Purchaser removes the collateral, and the S/P does not re-file the F/S within 4 Months after it enters the new state, perfection or will be lost (as per §9-103)
- Requirements to be Classified as a BIOC: (§1-201(9) and §9-307(1))
    - Ordinary Purchase - must be from *inventory*
    - New Value - not good enough to cancel an old debt with it
    - Good Faith
    - No knowledge that it is *violating* another S/A
    - Buys from Debtor - he cannot buy from a Non-BIOC Purchaser

- Since the BIOC must buy from the Debtor himself, if a Purchaser buys used equipment (thereby attaining Non-BIOC status) and sells it as inventory in his used equipment shop, the Buyer (who may have bought in Good Faith, for New Value, and Without Knowledge of a violation) will NOT take free of the original S/I.
- Since a BIOC takes free, any transferee thereafter takes free, even if the transferee knows that its in violation of the original agreement (Note: 2nd Cir. says Transferee does not take free)
- Non-BIOCs will take free of any Future Advances (covered by the S/A) made <u>45 Days</u> *after* the purchase
- <u>Non-BIOCs who use secured goods as security for themselves:</u>
    - If a Purchaser buys Equipment from a Debtor (while the Equipment is perfected by S/P), the Purchaser may still use this equipment as collateral to secure a loan for himself.
    - **Limitation**: The Buyer's Creditors may only secure the "leftover" interest in the equipment (i.e. whatever remains left after the Seller's (the original Debtor) Creditor (the original S/P) disposes of it.)
- Note: §9-306(2) ("Continuation in Proceeds for Non-BIOCS") applies <u>unless</u> the sale is authorized (it usually is assumed with inventory).

RELEVANT RULES: 1-201(9); 9-307; 9-309

§1-201(9): Buyer In The Ordinary Course Of Business:

1. A "Buyer In The Ordinary Course" ("BIOC") is an Individual/Organization (not a pawnbroker) who buys goods:
   - a) In Good Faith (see §1-201(19))
   - and b) Without knowledge that purchase is in violation of someone else's S/I (or other ownership rights)
   - and c) From a 'Merchant' - someone in the business of selling *those* goods (except a pawnbroker)
   - and d) In the *Ordinary Course* - passing of title *for value* (i.e. a sale) in a typical transaction (ex: inventory, not equipment)
   - and e) For **Value**

2. Anyone selling minerals, oil, or gas (at wellhead or minehead) is considered to be in the business of selling goods of that kind.

3. How Goods May Be Bought:
   - a) For Cash
   - or b) By Exchange of property
   - or c) On Credit - secured or unsecured
   - or d) Receiving goods/title under a pre-existing contract for sale

4. Goods are NOT considered Bought if:
   - a) They are given as a security for a debt
   - b) They are given as partial or total satisfaction of a debt
   - c) They are Bulk Transfer

§9-307: Protection Of Buyers Of Goods:

(1) A BUYER IN THE ORDINARY COURSE OF BUSINESS
- a) A "BIOC" takes FREE of any S/I even if
  - 1) The S/I is perfected
  - and 2) The buyer knows of its existence
- b) **Requirement:** The S/I must have been created by the seller (i.e. the seller must be the original Debtor)
- c) Exception: This section does not apply to people buying farm products from a person engaged in farming operations.

(2) CONSUMER GOODS (Consumer to Consumer):Buyer takes free and clear if
- a) He buys without knowledge of S/I
- and b) He buys for Value
- and c) He buys it for his own personal, family, or household use
- and d) The S/P did not file a financing statement *before* consumer purchased

(3) OTHER BUYERS: (Not Ordinary Course of Business):
- a) A Buyer takes free of Future Advances covered by a S/I only if the Future Advances are made *before* the *earlier* of:
  - 1. The time that the S/P acquires knowledge of the purchases
  - or 2. 45 Days after the purchase
- b) A Buyer will NOT take free of Future Advances if they are made Pursuant to a Commitment entered into:
  - 1. Without knowledge of the purchase
  - and 2. Before the expiration of the 45 day period

§9-309: Protection Of Purchasers Of Instruments, Documents, And Securities:

1. Article 9 does NOT limit the rights of a:
   - a) Holder In Due Course of a Negotiable Instrument (§3-302)
   - or b) Holder to whom a Negotiable Document has been duly Negotiated (§7-501)
   - or c) A *Protected Purchaser* of a security (§8-303)
2. Such Holders or Purchasers Take Priority over an *earlier* (and, of course, later), S/I (even if perfected).
3. Filing under Article 9 does NOT constitute Notice to such holders/Purchasers.

B. BANKRUPTCY

OVERVIEW

- Overall View:
  - The moment the Debtor files its Bankruptcy petition, a "lien" is created on every piece of collateral in the Debtor's possession *("Avoidance Powers")*
  - An **"Automatic Stay"** is created, thereby "freezing" the Debtor's property, so that nothing can be disposed of, transferred, attached or perfected.
  - The Trustee or DIP ("Debtor in Possession") becomes the Lien Creditor; but, as with most liens, a Lien Creditor cannot take priority over a perfected Secured Party (§9-301(1)(b))
  - The court must therefore determine who is perfected. To do this, we must determine at what date the Secured Party perfected. He must have perfected *before* the **Preference Period** in order to maintain priority; There are exceptions to this rule in the "**Savings Clauses**" (See §547(c))
  - Secured Parties entitled to priority of the collateral may take their collateral by convincing the court to "**Lift the Automatic Stay**"

- General Problems in Bankruptcy: In order to remain a Secured Creditor, one must overcome:
  - Avoidance Powers
  - and • Preferences
  - and • Fraudulent Transfers
  - and • Automatic Stay
- Note: **Erroneous filing in the correct state** (as per §9-401(3)) will not protect one from the Trustee; it only protects one from other Secured Ptys.

- Preferences:
  - One must examine the following questions before determining if a transfer was a Preference:
  - When was date of transfer (§547(e))?
  - Are ALL the elements of §547(b) fulfilled?
  - Do any §547(c) exceptions apply?
  - Was it sold to an insider?

- **"Floating Liens":**
  - Floating Liens usually occur when dealing with Inventory or Accounts Receivable (A/R) securities including After-Acquired property (since they are expected to be constantly turned over).
  - Since After-Acquired property is often covered by a S/A, §547(c)(5) allows it to be exempt from the voidable preference laws to a certain extent. In order to determine the value of the collateral on which the creditor remains secured, a simple formula can be applied. The formula will show how much of the value of the collateral the creditor may keep, and how much of the collateral's value it must return to the Bankruptcy estate:

FORMULA:

1. **Amount Creditor May Keep =**

> Total Collateral Value Bkcy date
> \- Amount Which Must Be Returned

2. **Amount Which Must Be Returned =**

> (Loan Value "S/I Date" - Collateral Value "S?I Date")
> \- (Loan Value date of Bkcy petition (Including Voidable Preference Payments)
> \- Collateral Value date of Bkcy petition)

3. **"S/I Date"** - for purposes of this formula, shall be the *Later* of:
   a) 90 Days before Bankruptcy
   or b) The Date value was *first given* under the S/A

4. *Restrictions of Formula:*
   a) The Amount which must be returned can never be negative (if it is, it considered zero)
   b) The Loan Value must always be ≥ the Collateral Value (if it is not, the Creditor may keep the entire value of the collateral)

- **PMSI's:** Since PMSI's are usually considered "contemporaneous," they can often be "saved" under §547(c)(1) or (3).

RELEVANT RULES: BC 544; 546; 547; 548

§544: Avoiding Powers:

(a) Trustee's Avoidance Powers:

- i) At commencement of the case, the trustee shall have the
  1. Rights and powers of any Creditor
  2. Right to avoid any transfer of debtor's property
  3. Right to avoid any obligation incurred by the Debtor
- ii) These powers are received regardless of the trustee or any Creditor knowledge
- ii) Scope of Voidability: Avoidance powers apply to obligations/transfers that are voidable by:
  - (1) A Creditor that:
    - a) Extends credit to Debtor by petition date
    - and b) Obtains a Judicial Lien with respect to such credit
      1. At petition date
      - and 2. On all property on which a Creditor on a simple contract could have obtained such a judicial lien -- regardless of whether a Creditor actually exists (i.e. a "Hypothetical Lien Creditor")
  - or (2) A Creditor that:
    - a) Extends credit to Debtor by petition date
    - and b) Obtains an execution against the Debtor that is returned unsatisfied -- regardless of its actual existence (i.e. "Hypothetical Lien Creditor")
  - or (3) A Bona-Fide Purchaser of Real Property (other than fixtures) that buys from a Debtor:
    - a) Against whom applicable law permits such transfer to be perfected
    - b) That obtains the status of Bona-Fide Purchaser
    - c) Who has a perfected such transfer by petition date - regardless of whether or not such a purchaser actually exists (i.e. "Hypothetical Lien Creditor")

(b) The Trustee may Avoid:

1. Any transfer of interest of the Debtor in property

or 2. Any obligation/debt incurred by the Debtor that is

a. Avoidable (under applicable law) by an unsecured Creditor under §502

or b. Not allowable only under §502(e)

§546: Exceptions To Avoiding Powers:

(a) An action (under §544,545,547,548,or 553) must be commenced *after* the earlier of:

(1) 2 Yrs. after Trustee's appointment

(2) The time the case is closed or dismissed

(b) Trustee's avoidance powers are subject to:

1) Any generally applicable law permitting perfection to relate-back in time (thereby allowing a later S/I to be effective against an earlier interest in the same property)

2) An interest in property shall be perfected by notice if

a) Such law dictates that perfection can only be accomplished by *either:*

1. Seizure of property

or 2. Commencement of an action

and b) There has been no seizure or commencement by petition date

3) Notice must be made within the time fixed by such law requiring seizure or commencement (for perfection)

(c) Reclamation Rights:

The rights and powers of a trustee (under §544(a), 545, 547, and 549) are subject to any rights (Statutory or Common Law) of a *Seller of Goods* to reclaim goods sold to Debtor.

(1) **Requirements:**

a. Goods are sold in the Ordinary Course of Seller's Business

and b. Debtor received goods while insolvent

and c. Seller makes a written demand within 10 Days after Debtor receives goods

(2) Seller's Right to Reclamation may be denied if court

(A) Grants seller's claim under §503(b)

or (B) Secures seller's claim by a lien

(d) Crops * * *

(e, f) Trustee Cannot avoid Margin Payments * * *

(g) Trustee Cannot avoid "Swap Agreements" * * *

§547: Preferences:

(a) Definitions (Note: These definitions apply to the bankruptcy provisions.)

(1) **"Inventory"** - Personal Property which is:
- a. Leased or furnished
- b. Held for sale or lease
- c. To be furnished under a contract for service
- d. Raw Materials
- e. Work-in-process
- f. Materials used or consumed in business
- g. Farm products held for lease (such as crops or livestock)

(2) **"New Value"** -
- a) This includes:
  - 1) Money
  - 2) Money's worth in goods, services or new credit
  - 3) Release by a transferee of property (which was previously transferred to it in a valid transaction by the Debtor (or trustee under applicable law)) including Proceeds of such property.
- b) An obligation substituted for an existing obligation is not considered New Value.

(3) **"Receivable"** - a right to payment (whether or not such right has been earned by performance)

(4) A Debt for a tax is incurred on the day when such tax is last payable *without penalty* (including any extensions).

(b) Voidable Preferences: A Trustee may Avoid any transfer of interest of the Debtor, in property which is:

(1) To or for the benefit of a Creditor

and (2) For/on account of an *Antecedent Debt* (i.e. past debt owed by Debtor before transfer was made; not a contemporaneous transaction (under §547(c)(1)))

and (3) Made while the Debtor was insolvent (under 547 (f))

and (4) Made *either:*

(A) Within 90 Days of petition date

or (B) Between 90 Days to 1 Year of petition date for "*Insiders*" (as per BRC §101)

and (5) A transfer that enables the Creditor to receive more than he would if:

(A) The case were under Chapter 7 (Liquidation; i.e. the Creditor is not over-secured under §725)

and (B) The transfer had not been made

and (C) Creditor received payment of debt under this title

(c) **Exceptions:** (Savings Clauses)

(1) Contemporaneous Exchanges: Transactions will be considered contemporaneous *to the extent* that they were *both*:

(A) Intended to be a ***Contemporaneous Exchange*** for **New Value** (ex: a check which is cashed within 30 days after it is exchanged is considered contemporaneous)

and (B) In fact a *Substantially* contemporaneous exchange (see 547(e))

(2) Ordinary Course of Business: Transfers qualify if:

(A) It was a payment of a Debt that was incurred in the *Ordinary Course of Business*

and (B) It was made in the *Ordinary Course of Business* or financial affairs of the Debtor and the Transferee (ex: regular Bond payments, regular installments on a loan)

and (C) Made according to Ordinary Business Terms

(3) PMSI's: Qualify only if:
  (A) The S/I secures *New Value* that was:
    (i) Given At or After signing a S/A (S/A must contain description of new collateral)
    and (ii) Given by the Secured Pty
    and (iii) Given as a PMSI (i.e. to enable Debtor to acquire property)
    and (iv) Was actually used by Debtor to acquire property (i.e. a "true PMSI").
  and (B) It was Perfected within 20 Days after the Debtor receives possession of the property

(4) New Value: A transfer given to the Creditor who gave *New Value* **after** Debtor made the transfer, if:
  (A) The new value was not secured by an *unavoidable* (i.e. not perfected) S/I (and therefore subject to the avoiding powers under §546)
  (B) The Debtor did not make the Creditor better off than he would have been if the Creditor did not give the Debtor new value (ex: over secures, to extend to past debts)

(5) Floating Liens: New **Perfected** S/I's in Inventory or Receivable *including their proceeds*: As long as the S/I does not prejudice unsecured creditors by "over-securing" to cover debts made during the LATER of:
  (A) *Either:*
    (i) 90 Days before the petition date (for a transfer applying to §547(b)(4)(A))
    or (ii) 1 Year before the petition date, if the transfer was made by an *"insider"* (as per §547(b)(4)(B))
  (B) The date that *New Value* was first given under the S/A to create the S/I

(6) Unavoidable Statutory Liens (pursuant to §545) (ex: statutory liens)
(7) Payments to Ex-Spouse * * *
(8) Property of a Personal Debtor if:
  a) Debtor's debts are primarily Consumer Debts
  and b) The total value of all affected transferred property is < $600

(d) Avoiding Transfers to a Surety

1) The trustee may avoid a transfer of an interest in the Debtor's property which is to or for the benefit of a Surety if:

a) It is to secure reimbursement of such a Surety

and b) The Surety furnished a bond or other obligation to dissolve a Judicial Lien (which the trustee could have avoided under §547(b)).

2) The liability of the Surety under such a bond/obligation shall be *discharged* to the extent of *either:*

a) The value of such property recovered by the trustee

or b) The amount paid to the trustee

(e) **Time of Transfer** (for purposes of this section)

(1) **Perfection:**

(A) **Real Property** (other than fixtures): Perfection occurs when a *Bona-Fide Purchaser* who buys from the debtor (against whom applicable law permits such a transfer to be perfected) cannot acquire an interest that is superior to that of the Secured Pty (i.e. when the transaction is recorded).

(B) **Personal Property** (including fixtures): Perfection occurs when a Creditor cannot acquire a superior Judicial Lien to that of the Secured Pty (i.e. the S/I is perfected so that it is superior under UCC §9-301(1)(b)).

(2) **When Transfer is Made**:

(A) When transfer is actually made, if its perfected within 10 Days of transfer

or (B) Upon Perfection, if perfected **after** 10 days after transfer

or (C) Immediately before petition is filed If is NOT perfected by the *later* of:

(i) The commencement of the case (petition date)

or (ii) 10 Days after the transfer is actually made

(3) The Debtor must acquire rights in property for transfer to be made.

(f) Preference Period: Debtor is presumed to have been insolvent within 90 Days immediately preceding petition date (for purposes of this section)

(g) Burden of Proof: For purposes of this section,

1. The Trustee must prove avoidability of a transfer (under §547(b).

2. The Creditor (or party in interest against whom recovery or avoidance is sought) has the burden of proving non-avoidability under §547(c).

§548: Fraudulent Transfers:

(a) A Trustee may avoid Transfers made within 1 Yr. of petition date if the Debtor:

(1) Made the Transfer with Actual Intent to **Hinder, Delay** or **Defraud** any other Creditors (including those created after transfer)

or (2) *Either:*

(A) Received *less than reasonably equivalent value* (in exchange for the transfer/obligation)

and (B) The Debtor was *either:*

(i) Insolvent *either*

1) As a result of transfer/obligation

or 2) When the transfer was made

or (ii) Undercapitalized

or (iii) Creditor knew or should have known Debtor couldn't "afford" the transfer

(b) Trustee of a Partnership - A Trustee can generally avoid transfers by an insolvent partnership to a General Partner if the debtor was insolvent when the transfer was made (or became insolvent as a result of the transfer).

(c) Exception: Unless a Trustee can avoid the transfer (under §544,545,546, or 547), a creditor may avoid a transfer if it takes the Transfer or Obligation:

1) For New Value
2) In Good Faith
3) For a "fair" price

(d) (1) **Time of Transfer** (for purposes of this section):

a) A Transfer is made when it is so perfected that even a Bona-Fide Purchaser who buys from the Debtor (against whom applicable law permits such a transfer to be perfected) cannot acquire an interest superior to that of the Transferee.

b) If such a transfer is not so perfected (as indicated above) before the petition date, then the transfer will be deemed to have been made immediately before the date of the filing of the petition.

(2) Other Terms * * *

VI. DEFAULT

1. REMEDY: DISPOSAL

OVERVIEW

- Remedy: Generally, a S/P may repossess his collateral upon Debtor's default; but he must SELL the collateral and take only the amount of money he is secured for.

- Upon default, all outstanding debt payments become "*accelerated*" (i.e. due immediately), unless otherwise agreed.

- The S/P may keep the collateral instead of selling it if neither the debtor nor any other creditors object to the S/P's proposal (See §9-505(a)).

- If something is leased or consigned, it need not be sold since the "Creditor" (the "Lessor" or "Consignor") is deemed to own the property (i.e. no debt is owed, just return on property).

- A S/P may take all the money he has advanced which is secured by particular collateral, as long he was "*first to file or perfect*" (see Future Advances); (ex: if A perfects a S/I in a car for $5,000, on Day 1 and B perfects a S/I in the car for $8,000 on Day 5, A maintains Priority; Even if A advances another $6,000 on Day 8 - after B perfected - A is entitled to $11,000 before B can collect his $8,000).

RELEVANT RULES: 9-501; 9-502; 9-503; 9-504; 9-505; 9-506; 9-507

§9-501: Rights and Remedies of Parties Upon Default:

(1) **S/P's Right's and Remedies**:

a. When a Debtor is in Default under a S/A, the Secured Pty has rights and remedies provided by this Part.

b. The S/P's rights and remedies may be expanded in the S/A, yet, these rights will be subject to §9-501(3).

c. S/P's Available Remedies

1. Reduce his claim to judgment

or 2. Foreclose

or 3. Enforce the S/I by any available judicial procedure

or 4. If collateral is Documents, he may proceed as to the documents *or* goods covered by them.

d. A S/P in possession of collateral has rights, remedies, and duties as provided by §9-207

e. The remedies listed above are cumulative (i.e. they may be used together)

(2) **Debtor's Rights and Remedies:** Upon default, the Debtor has rights and remedies as provided by:

a. This Part

and b. The S/A

and c. §9-207

(3) **Non-Waivable Rights and Duties**

i) **Rights and Duties Which Cannot be Waived:**

(a) S/P's duty to Account for any Surplus Proceeds of Collateral (§9-502(2) and §9-504(2)).

(b) Rights and Duties concerning Disposition of Collateral (§9-504(3) and §9-505(1)).

(c) Rights and Duties concerning Acceptance of Collateral as Discharge of Obligation (§9-505(2)) ("Strict Foreclosure").

(d) Rights to Redeem Collateral (§9-506).

(e) S/P's liability for failure to comply with these Default rules (as per §9-507(1)).

ii) The rules listed above cannot be waived since they require the S/P to perform special duties and give the Debtor special rights.

iii) **Exceptions** - The above Rights and Duties may be waived or changed when dealing with:

a) *Compulsory Disposition of Collateral* (as per §9-504(3) and §9-505)

or b) *Redemption of Collateral* (as per §9-506)

iv) Standards of Measurement: The parties may determine, by agreement, the *standards* by which these rights and duties are to be measured - as long as those standards are *not manifestly unreasonable*.

(4) If the S/A covers both Real Property and Personal Property, the S/P may *either:*

a) Proceed under the UCC (Article 9, Part 5) only for the Personal Property

or b) Proceed under the State's Real Property law for both Personal and Real Property (in which case, this Part does not apply)

(5) **Judicial Lien or Sale**:

a. When a S/P has reduced his claim to judgment, the Judicial Lien of a Levy made upon his collateral (for his benefit) will *Relate Back* to the date of Perfection of the S/I (in the collateral)

b. Judicial Sale

1. A Judicial Sale is considered to be a "Foreclosure of the S/I by judicial procedure" (within the meaning of this section).
2. The S/P may purchase his collateral at the sale.
3. If the S/P buys the collateral, he may take it free of any other requirements of Article 9.

§9-502: Collection Rights Of Secured Parties:

(1) In the event of Default, or when so agreed, the S/P may:

a. Notify the Account Debtor (or the Obligor on an Instrument) to make payment to him for the outstanding debt (regardless of who was collecting payment for the indebtedness)

or b. Take Control of any Proceeds which he is entitled to (under §9-306)

(2) S/P's Options:

a. The S/P may, *by agreement*:

1. Be entitled to charge back uncollected collateral

or 2. Have full or limited recourse against the Debtor

or 3. Undertake to collect from the Account Debtor or Obligors

b. If the S/P is entitled to any of the above options,

1. He must proceed in a *Commercially Reasonable Manner*

and 2. He may deduct his reasonable expenses of realization from the collections

c. If the S/A secures an indebtedness

1. The S/P must Account (i.e. return) to the Debtor for any Surplus

and 2. The Debtor will be liable for any deficiency (unless otherwise agreed)

d. **Exception:** The Debtor will not be liable for any Deficiency and the S/P will not be obligated to return any Surplus if:

1. If the S/A does not specifically require

and 2. The underlying transaction is *either*

a) Sale of **Accounts**

or b) Sale of **Chattel Paper**

§9-503: Secured Party's Right To Take Possession After Default:

1) The S/P has a right to take possession of collateral upon default (unless otherwise agreed).
2) The S/P may proceed to take possession without judicial action if it can be done *"without breach of the peace."*
3) The Security Agreement may require the Debtor to make the collateral available to the S/P at a designated, mutually convenient place.
4) A S/P may render Equipment unusable or dispose of collateral (as per §9-504) on the debtor's premises if it cannot be removed.

§9-504: Secured Party's Right To Dispose After Default:

(1) Disposition of Collateral:

i) Upon default, a S/P may sell, lease, or otherwise dispose of collateral, *either:*

a. In its present condition

or b. Following any *commercially reasonable Preparation or Processing*

ii) Any sale of goods is subject to the Article on Sales (Article 2)

iii) Proceeds of the disposition shall be applied in the order of the following:

(a) **Selling Expenses** - the reasonable expenses of retaking, holding, preparing for sale/lease, and selling/leasing (including reasonable attorney/legal expenses involved (to the extend provided for by S/A (and not prohibited by law)))

(b) **Satisfaction of Debt** - under his Security Agreement

(c) **Satisfaction of other Debts** - secured by any *Subordinate* S/I holders if:

1) Written notice of demand is received before distribution of the proceeds is completed

and 2) Reasonable proof of S/I is presented (upon S/P's request)

(2) Deficiency and Surplus:

a) If the S/I secures an Indebtedness, then, **unless otherwise agreed**:

1) The Debtor is entitled to surplus of the sale from the S/P

and 2) The S/P (seller) is entitled to deficiency from the Debtor

b) If the underlying transaction was a Sale of Accounts or Chattel Paper then, **ONLY if the Security Agreement provides**:

1) Debtor is entitled to surplus of the sale from the S/P

and 2) S/P (seller) is entitled to deficiency from the Debtor

(3) Notice of Disposition:

a) Disposition may be made by public or private proceedings.

b) Disposition may be made as a one whole sale, or in separate transactions (under separate contracts).

c) Disposition sale must be made under any *commercially reasonable* terms (including the method, manner, time, and place of the sale)

d) S/P is not required to sell all collateral to one party.

e) Secured Pty must notify Debtor of time and place of sale *unless:*

1) Debtor agrees not to be notified after default

or 2) Collateral is perishable

or 3) Collateral is very sensitive to market (value changes quickly)

or 4) Collateral is of a type customarily sold on a recognized market

f) Notification:

1) For *Consumer Goods*, no other notification must be sent

2) For all other goods, notification must be sent to all other Secured Ptys who sent Selling S/P a written notice of claim of an interest in the collateral.

g) The S/P may purchase the collateral:

1) At any **Public Sale**

or 2) At a **Private Sale**, if

a. The collateral is of the type sold in a recognized market

or b. The collateral is of a type which is subject to a widely distributed standard price quotation

(4) Even if the Secured Pty files to make a proper sale, a Purchaser takes Free of the S/P's (and any other subordinate's) right/interest in the collateral if:

(a) Collateral sold public sale:

1) Collateral is sold at a Public Sale.

and 2) Purchaser has no knowledge of any defects in sale process.

and 3) Purchaser does not buy in collusion with another Secured Pty, the person conducting the sale, or other bidders.

and (b) The Purchaser acts in Good Faith (in all other sales (i.e. private sale)).

(5) Non-Qualifying Sales or Dispositions:

a) A Person has rights and duties of a S/P if:

1) She is liable to a S/P under either a:

a. Guaranty

or b. Indorsement

or c. Repurchase Agreement

or d. The like

and 2) She *either:*

a. Receives a transfer of collateral from the S/P

or b. Is subrogated to her rights

b) Such a transfer of collateral is not considered to be a "Sale or Disposition of Collateral" under Article 9.

§9-505: Disposition Of Collateral:

(1) Compulsory Disposition Of Collateral

a) A S/P who has taken possession of the collateral must dispose of it under §9-504 within 90 Days after he takes possession if:

1) The Debtor has paid 60% of *either:*

a. The cash price of a Consumer Goods PMSI

or b. The loan of any other S/I in Consumer Goods

and 2) The Debtor has not signed a statement after default, renouncing or modifying his rights under this Part

b) If the S/P does not dispose of the collateral (pursuant to §9-504) within <u>90 Days</u>, the Debtor may recover on the S/P's liability either
  1) In conversion
  or 2) Under §9-507(1)

(2) <u>Acceptanee of Collateral as Discharge of Obligation</u>

a) In all other cases (not specified in §9-505(1)) the S/P may propose to retain the collateral as Discharge of debtor's obligation (i.e. Strict Foreclosure)

b) <u>Notice:</u>
  1) If the Debtor has not signed a statement renouncing or modifying his rights under this subsection, the S/P shall, after default send <u>written</u> notice of his proposal (to keep the collateral in satisfaction of the debt).
  2) **Additional Notice:**
    a. <u>Consumer Goods:</u> No other notice is required
    b. <u>Other Cases</u>: S/P must send a copy of the notice to all other Secured Parties who:
      1. Have sent the S/P a <u>written</u> notice of their claim to interest in the collateral
      and 2. S/P has *received* the notice *<u>before</u> either:*
        i) The Debtor renounced or modified its rights
        or ii) S/P sends Debtor notice to accept collateral as discharge.
  3) If anyone entitled to receive notice (including Debtor) objects to the S/P's proposal within <u>21 Days</u> after notice was *sent*, S/P must dispose of the collateral (under §9-504).
  4) The S/P may keep the collateral in satisfaction of the Debtor's obligation if he does not receive any written objection (within <u>21 days</u>).

§9-506: Debtor's Right To Redeem Collateral:

1) Unless otherwise agreed in writing, after default, the Debtor or any other Secured Pty may redeem the collateral at any time *before*:
   - a) The S/P has disposed of the collateral
   - and b) The S/P has entered into a contract for the collateral's disposition (as per §9-504)
   - and c) The obligation has been discharged (as per §9-505(2))

2. The party redeeming the collateral must pay
   - a) *All* of the obligations secured by the collateral (i.e. debt is "accelerated," and debtor must pay all of his debt, not just the missed installments)
   - and b) Expenses *reasonably incurred* by the Secured Pty while
     - 1) Retaking the collateral
     - and 2) Holding the collateral
     - and 3) Preparing the collateral for disposition
     - and 4) Arranging for the sale
   - and c) Reasonable attorney fees and legal expenses (to the extent provided in the agreement, and not prohibited by law)

§9-507: Secured Party's Liability For Failure To Comply:

(1) If it is established that the S/P is not proceeding in accordance with this Part, then:

a. If Disposition has not occurred - it may be ordered or restrained (i.e. by legal action, on appropriate terms and conditions)

b. If Disposition has already occurred - the following parties may recover *any loss caused* by S/P's failure to comply with this part:

1. The Debtor

or 2. Any party entitled to notification

or 3. Any party whose S/I had been made known to the S/P before the disposition

c. If collateral is Consumer Goods, the Debtor has a right to recover:

1. An amount not less than:
The credit service charge + 10% of the principal amount of the debt

or 2. The time price differential + 10% of the cash price

(2) **Commercially Reasonable Manner**

a. The fact that a better price could have been obtained had the S/P chosen a different method or time for the sale, does not - of itself - prove that the sale wasn't made in a Commercially Reasonable Manner.

b. A S/P is deemed to have sold the collateral in a Commercially Reasonable Manner if:

1. The S/P sells the collateral in the usual manner in any recognized market

or 2. He sells it at the current Market Price (at the time of the sale)

or 3. He sells it in conformity with *recognized commercial practices* among Dealers in the type of property sold

or 4. The disposition is approved
   - a) In any Judicial Proceeding
   - b) By any Bona-fide Creditor's Committee
   - c) By any Representative of Creditors

(*** Note: Approval is not required for a disposition to be deemed Commercially Reasonable)

c. The above two rules also apply to other types of disposition when appropriate.

2. *SURPLUS/DEFICIENCY AFTER DISPOSITION*

OVERVIEW

- Normally:
    - The S/P is entitled to any Deficiency (i.e. if the sale of the collateral did not cover the amount of the debt covered by the S/I).

  and
    - The Debtor is entitled to any Surplus (i.e. if the S/P sold the collateral for more than Debtor's outstanding debt)

- **Exceptions:**
    - The S/P will not have to return any surplus nor will the debtor have to pay for any deficiency (unless the S/A explicitly indicates otherwise) if the underlying transaction was a sale of **Accounts or Chattel Paper** (§9-502(2)).

    - The Debtor will not be liable for deficiency (although S/P will be have to return any surplus) if the collateral is not owned by the Debtor (unless the S/A explicitly indicates otherwise) (§9-112).

RELEVANT RULES: 9-502(2); 9-504(2); 9-112

§9-502(2): Collection Rights Of Secured Parties:

* * *

c. If the S/A secures an indebtedness
1. The S/P must Account (i.e. return) to the Debtor for any Surplus
and 2. The Debtor will be liable for any deficiency (unless otherwise agreed)

d. **Exception:** The Debtor will not be liable for any Deficiency and the S/P will not be obligated to return any Surplus if:
1. If the S/A does not specifically require
and 2. The underlying transaction is *either*
a) Sale of **Accounts**
or b) Sale of **Chattel Paper**

§9-504(2) Deficiency and Surplus:

a) If the S/I secures an Indebtedness, then, **unless otherwise agreed**:
1) The Debtor is entitled to surplus of the sale from the S/P
and 2) The S/P (seller) is entitled to deficiency from the Debtor
b) If the underlying transaction was a Sale of Accounts or Chattel Paper then, **ONLY if the Security Agreement provides**:
1) Debtor is entitled to surplus of the sale from the S/P
and 2) S/P (seller) is entitled to deficiency from the Debtor

§9-112: Where Collateral Is Not Owned By Debtor:

When a S/P knows that collateral is not owned by the Debtor, then, unless otherwise agreed, the Owner of the collateral:
1) Is entitled to receive any surplus from disposition (under §9-502(2) or §9-504(1))
2) Is not liable for any deficiency after resale

3. *DEBTOR'S RIGHTS*

A. *Requests For Statements*

RELEVANT RULES: 9-208; 9-404; 9-406

§9-208: Request For A Statement Of Account Or List Of Collateral:

(1) **Confirming outstanding debt:**

a) A Debtor may send a S/P a signed statement indicating the total amount he believes he owes (to a S/P as of a specified date), requesting that the S/P confirm or correct the stated balance.

b) Debtor may also send the S/P a list of collateral to approve or correct (if the agreement (or other record) specifically identifies the collateral).

(2) **Answering The Request:**

a) Secured Pty must send a written approval or correction within 2 weeks.

b) If S/P claims a S/I in all of a particular type of collateral (ex: inventory), he only needs to indicate that he does (no need to approve each item separately).

c) **Failure to comply:** If S/P fails to reply (without reasonable excuse):

1) He is liable for any resulting loss caused to the Debtor.

2) He is limited to the collateral listed in the Debtor's confirmation against persons *misled by his failure to comply* if the Debtor properly included:

a. A *Good Faith Statement of his obligation*

or b. A list of the collateral

d) If the S/P no longer has the S/I (i.e. he assigned it):

1) He must disclose the name and address of the new Secured Pty (if known to him)

and 2) He is liable for any loss caused to the Debtor as a result of failing to disclose (as per §9-208)

e) Successors of interest are not obligated to reply unless they personally received a request.

(3) The Debtor is entitled to such a statement once every 6 Months, without charge (each additional statement may not exceed a $10.00 charge).

§9-404: The Termination Statement:

(1) **Demanding the Termination Statement**

a. **Consumer Goods**:

1. The S/P must **File** a Termination Statement (wherever he filed a F/S) within 1 Month or within 10 Days after S/P receives a Written demand for the Termination Statement if:
    - a) There is no outstanding Secured Obligation
    - and b) There is no commitment to make advances, incur obligations or give value
    - and c) The F/S covers Consumer Goods
    - and d) The original Financing Statement was filed after the effective date of the Revised Article 9
2. Each Termination Statement must:
    - a) State that the Secured Pty no longer claims a S/I under the F/S
    - and b) Include the Filing Number of the original F/S

b. **Other Cases** (Non-Consumer Goods):

1. Within 10 Days of Debtor's Written demand, the S/P must **Send** to the Debtor one Termination Statement for each F/S he filed
2. Each Termination Statement must
    - a) Include the Filing Number of the original F/S
    - and b) State that the Secured Pty no longer claims a S/I under the F/S
3. The S/P must only comply with Debtor's demand if:
    - a) There is no outstanding Secured Obligation
    - b) There is no commitment to make advances, incur obligations or give value

c. **Signature**:
1. The Termination Statement should be signed by the S/P.
2. A Termination Statement signed by another person will be valid only if:
   a) It is accompanied by a separate written Statement of Assignment, signed by the S/P
   and b) The Statement of Assignment complies with §9-405(2)
   and c) Payment of the required fee is included

d. **Penalty For Noncompliance**: If, upon Debtor's demand, the S/P fails to comply with this subsection, the S/P shall be liable for:
1. A $100 penalty
and 2. Any loss caused to the Debtor by S/P's failure to comply

(2) Filing The Termination Statement

a. Upon presentation, the Filing Officer must note the Termination Statement on the index.

b. If the officer has received 2 copies of the Termination Statement, he shall return the copy to the S/P, *stamped*, to show when it was received.

c. **Removal of records**
1. The Filing Officer may remove original records from the file at any time after the receipt of the Termination Statement *if* the Filing Officer has a copy (on microfilm or other photographic records) of the:
   a) Financing Statement
   and b) Continuation Statement
   and c) Statement of Assignment
   and d) Statement of Release

2. If there are No photographic records, the officer must wait at least 1 Year after receiving the Termination Statement before removing the originals from the files.

(3) **Filing Fee** * * *

§9-406: Release Of Collateral:

1) A S/P of Record may release all or part of any collateral described in a filed F/S by signing a **Statement of Release**

2) The Statement of Release must contain:
   a. A Description of the collateral being released
   and b. The name and address of the Debtor
   and c. The name and address of the Secured Pty of Record
   and d. The file number of the F/S

3) **Signature**
   a. The Statement of Release should be signed by the S/P
   b. A Statement of Release signed by another person will be valid only if:
      1) It is accompanied by a separate written Statement of Assignment, signed by the S/P of record
      and 2) The Statement of Assignment complies with §9-405(2)
      and 3) Payment of the required fee is included

4) **Filing the Release**
   a. Upon presentation of the Statement of Release, the Filing Officer shall:
      1. Mark the Release with the date and time of the filing
      and 2. Note the Release on the Index of the Financing Statement

   b. Fee for Filing the Release * * *

B. Using Collateral

RELEVANT RULES: 9-205

§9-205: Use Or Disposition Of Collateral Without An Accounting:

1) A S/I is NOT Invalid or Fraudulent, even if it:

a) Allows Debtor to:

1. Use, Commingle, or Dispose of all or part of the collateral

or 2. Collect or compromise Accounts or Chattel Paper

or 3. Accept returned goods

or 4. Make repossessions

or 5. Use, Commingle, or Dispose of Proceeds

or b) Does not require the Debtor to:

1. Account for proceeds

or 2. Replace collateral after disposition

2) This section does not relax the possession requirements for perfecting collateral.

C. Restraining Alienability

RELEVANT RULES: 9-311

§9-311: Alienability Of Debtor's Rights:

1) The Debtor's rights in the collateral may be *voluntarily* or *involuntarily* transferred by:

a) Sale
or b) Creation of another Security Interest
or c) Attachment
or d) Levy
or e) Garnishment
or f) Other Judicial Process

2) The Debtor may transfer his rights even if the S/A prohibits such a transfer or makes the transfer constitute a default.

4. S/P'S RIGHTS

- For S/P's rights upon default see "Default" above

RELEVANT RULES: 9-207; 9-317

§9-207: Secured Party's Rights And Duties Over Collateral In Its Possession:

(1) **Secured Parties Obligation:**

a) **General Collateral:** A S/P must use *Reasonable Care* in the custody and preservation of the collateral in its possession.

b) **Instruments and Chattel Paper**: *Reasonable Care* includes taking the necessary steps to preserve rights against prior parties (unless otherwise agreed).

(2) **Rights and Duties of the S/P:** Unless parties otherwise agree, the following rights and duties apply when the S/P has Possession of the collateral:

(a) Reasonable Expectations: A Secured Pty may charge the Debtor (and be secured for) any *Reasonable Expenses* (including insurance, taxes, and other charges) incurred in the:

1. Custody of the collateral

or 2. Preservation of the collateral

or 3. Operation/use of the collateral

(b) Risk of Loss: If Insurance proceeds are insufficient, the Debtor shall bear the risk of Accidental Loss or Damage of the collateral.

(c) Value from the Collateral:

1. **Non-Monetary:** The S/P may hold any increase in value or profits (except money) received from the collateral as additional security for the debt.
2. **Money:** Money received from the collateral (as profits from its increased value) shall *either* be:
   a) Returned to the Debtor
   or b) Applied in reduction of the secured debt

(d) Identification of Collateral: If the collateral is not fungible, the S/P must keep it *identifiable* (fungible property may be commingled (ex: grain)).

(e) Re-pledging: The S/P may re-pledge the collateral if it does not impair the debtor's rights to redeem it.

(3) Although the S/P will be liable for any loss caused by his failure to comply with the above obligations, he will not lose his S/I.

(4) **Use of Collateral:** A S/P may use or operate the collateral if it is:
a) For the purpose of preserving the collateral or its value
or b) Pursuant to a court order (in the appropriate jurisdiction)
or c) To the extent provided in the S/A (unless it's a Consumer Good)

§9-317: Secured Party Not Obligated On Contract Of Debtor:

A S/P does not incur Contract and Tort liability for the *Debtor's* acts or omissions, simply because of:
1) The mere existence of a S/I
or 2) The Authority given to the Debtor to dispose of or use the Collateral

SPECIAL CASES

I. CONSUMER GOODS

1. DEFINITION:

RELEVANT RULES: 9-109(1)

§9-109(1): Classification Of Goods:

Consumer Goods - goods used or bought primarily for personal, family, or household purposes.

- Note: Motor Vehicles are specifically excluded from Consumer Goods (see §9-302(1)(d))

2. ATTACHMENT:

OVERVIEW

- A written Security Agreement is required for attachment.
- "After-acquired property":
  - Consumer Goods: Can only cover After-Acquired property for goods acquired within 10 Days after the creation of the S/A
  - A S/A cannot cover After-Acquired **Household goods**

RELEVANT RULES: 9-204

§9-204(1), (2): After-Acquired Property; Future Advances:

(1) A S/A may provide for After-Acquired Property to secure the obligations covered by the S/A (except as provided below in (2)).

(2) **Consumer Goods Exception:**

a) After-Acquired Property will not attach to a S/I if:

1. The S/I is in Consumer Goods

and 2. The After-Acquired Property is given as *additional* security

b) Exceptions: After-Acquired Property will attach in Consumer Goods if:

1. Debtor acquires rights in the After-Acquired Property within 10 Days after the Secured Pty gave value

or 2. They are Accessions (see §9-314)

3. *PERFECTION: Automatic Perfection*

OVERVIEW

PMSI in Consumer Goods - no filing required

- A PMSI May be secured by anyone giving value for purchase (ex: seller or bank)
- Money must be Actually Used for the purchase of Consumer Goods
- Unlike regular perfection, the S/I is only in money given for purchase (initial money given; Future Advances are, thus, subject to intermediate liens)
- Security Agreement must be specific and signed by Debtor
- S/P must believe goods are to be used as Consumer Goods

RELEVANT RULES: 9-302(1)(d); 9-307(2)

§9-302(1)(d): Filing Not Required for Consumer Goods:

A PMSI in CONSUMER GOODS, unless it is for

1. Motor Vehicles required to be registered

or 2. Fixtures (as per §9-313)

§9-307(2): Protection Of Buyers Of Consumer Goods:

A Buyer of CONSUMER GOODS (Consumer to Consumer) takes free and clear if

a) He buys without knowledge of S/I

and b) He buys for Value

and c) He buys it for his own personal, family, or household use

and d) The S/P did not file a financing statement *before* consumer purchased

4. DISPOSITION:

RELEVANT RULES: 9-505(1); 9-507(1)

§9-505(1) Compulsory Disposition

A S/P who has taken possession of the collateral must dispose of it under §9-504 within 90 Days after he takes possession if:

1) The Debtor has paid 60% of *either:*
   a. The cash price of a Consumer Goods PMSI
   or b. The loan of any other S/I in Consumer Goods

and 2) The Debtor has not signed a statement after default, renouncing or modifying his rights under this Part

§9-507(1): Right to Recover for Failure to Comply

If it is established that the S/P is not proceeding in accordance with this Part, then If collateral is Consumer Goods, the Debtor has a right to recover:

1. An amount not less than:
   The credit service charge + 10% of the principal amount of the debt

or 2. The time price differential + 10% of the cash price

II. PMSI

1. DEFINITION:

RELEVANT RULES: 9-107

§9-107: Purchase Money Security Interest ("PMSI") :

A PMSI is a S/I which has been:

(a) Taken or retained by the **seller** of collateral to secure all/part of its price

or (b) Taken by a person who advances money (or incurs an obligation) that enables the Debtor to buy the collateral (ex: financing bank) (Note: Money must be used to buy goods in order for the S/I to be effective as a PMSI)

2. ATTACHMENT:

By Security Agreement

3. *PERFECTION:*

OVERVIEW

- PMSI in Consumer Goods - no filing required
    - A PMSI be secured by anyone giving value for purchase (ex: seller or bank)
    - Money must be Actually Used for the purchase of Consumer Goods
    - Unlike regular perfection, the S/I is only in money given for purchase (initial money given; Future Advances are, thus, subject to intermediate liens)
    - Security Agreement must be specific and signed by Debtor
    - S/P must believe goods are to be used as Consumer Goods
    - Note: Motor Vehicles are *specifically excluded* from Consumer Goods (see §9-302(1)(d))
- PMSI in goods: **10 days to perfect**
- PMSI in instruments: **21 days to perfect**

RELEVANT RULES: 9-302(1)(d); 9-103(1)(c)

§9-302(1)(d): Filing Not Required to Perfect a PMSI in Consumer Goods

A PMSI in <u>CONSUMER GOODS</u>, unless it is for

1. Motor Vehicles required to be registered

or 2. Fixtures (as per §9-313)

§9-103(1)(c): Perfecting Documents, Instruments, and Ordinary Goods in PMSIs in Multistate Transactions:

If parties creating a <u>PMSI</u> **understand**, *at the time the S/I attaches*, that the goods will be kept in another jurisdiction (i.e. the "proposed jurisdiction"), then the law of the jurisdiction <u>where goods are to be taken</u> applies:

1) Proposed Jurisdiction's laws apply from the time attachment occurs.
2) If goods are actually taken to their proposed jurisdiction, those laws remain in effect.
3) If the goods do not end up in their proposed jurisdiction then the proposed jurisdiction's laws apply for <u>30 Days</u> from the date of **possession by Debtor**.

4. PROCEEDS:

OVERVIEW

- PMSI Priority - If a S/I in Inventory was a PMSI, §9-312(3)'s super-priority gives the "Purchase Money" Secured Pty priority in the Cash Proceeds (non-cash proceeds will be subject to "first-to-file or perfect" rule), ONLY IF the **Cash** proceeds were received on or before Debtor delivers inventory to Third Pty buyer (i.e. to qualify, purchases must be COD or Pre-paid by purchaser; Purchases made on credit are not included in this exception).

5. PMSI PRIORITY:

RELEVANT RULES: 9-301(2); 9-312 (3),(4)

§9-301(2): PMSI Exception To Unsecured Priorities:

A Secured Pty takes priority over any Lien Creditor or "Bulk Transferee" (whose rights arise between the time of attachment and filing) if the Secured Pty files a PMSI:

a) Before Debtor receives the collateral (i.e. before attachment)

or b) Within 10 Days after Debtor receives **Possession** of the collateral

§9-312(3),(4): Priorities in PMSI's

(3) **PMSI Super-Priority in INVENTORY:**

i) A Perfected PMSI in inventory has Priority over a conflicting S/I in the same inventory.

ii) PMSI "Super-Priority" applies Only to:

a) The same inventory

and b) Identifiable **cash proceeds** received on or before the day that Debtor delivers the inventory to a Third Pty buyer (OK if proceeds are money, checks, deposit accounts; No good if converted to cash proceeds; must be direct cash proceeds (ex: car-trade-ins are not good, Accounts receivable and Chattel Paper are also no good))

iii) Requirements for PMSI Priority

(a) The PMSI is perfected when Debtor receives possession of inventory.

and (b) The "Purchase Money" Secured Pty *gives written notice* to the conflicting Secured Pty only if the conflicting Secured Pty filed a financing statement covering the same types of inventory *before:*

(i) The "Purchase Money" Secured Pty filed (or Debtor receives Possession)

or (ii) The beginning of the 21 Day period (in which a PMSI is temporarily perfected without filing or possession (as per §9-304(5)))

and (c) The Conflicting Secured Pty received the notification within 5 Yrs before the Debtor receives possession of the inventory (i.e. since a notice is effective for 5 Yrs, S/P can continue making PMSI's without further notices within 5 yr. period)

and (d) The notice states that the person sending it expects to obtain a PMSI in the debtor's Inventory (describing the inventory by or type)

(4) **A PMSI in Non-Inventory Collateral** (ex: Equipment):

A Purchase-Money-Secured Pty has priority over conflicting secured parties in collateral or its proceeds if the:

a. PMSI is perfected at the time Debtor receives possession of the collateral

or b. PMSI is perfected within 10 Days after Debtor receives possession of collateral

6. ***PMSI IN BANKRUPTCY:***

RELEVANT RULES: BC 547(c)(3)

Bankruptcy §547(c)(3): PMSI's Not Considered a Preference:

PMSI's: Qualify only if:

(A) The S/I secures *New Value* that was:

(i) Given At or After signing a S/A (S/A must contain description of new collateral)

and (ii) Given by the Secured Pty

and (iii) Given as a PMSI (i.e. to enable Debtor to acquire property)

and (iv) Was actually used by Debtor to acquire property (i.e. a "true PMSI").

and (B) It was Perfected within 20 Days after the Debtor receives possession of the property

III. LEASES

(see §1-201(37))

1. *ATTACHMENT:*

Lease agreement

2. *PERFECTION:*

OVERVIEW

- No need to perfect a lease agreement
- Best to file anyway - just in case it is considered to be a S/I
    - File where Debtor is located (for residual of collateral, especially with Chattel Paper)
    - File where leased property is (for present interest)

3. *PRIORITY:*

Must determine if the transaction is a Lease or a Security Agreement to determine priority

4. LEASE v. SECURITY INTEREST

OVERVIEW

- Important distinction because if the agreement is a lease, "lessor" retains equity, and he is not subject to any of "lessee's" creditors; If it is found to be a S/T - in substance - "Lessor" takes subject to "lessee's" creditors and must be filed to perfect a S/I in it.
- Court's look at the <u>Substance</u> of Agreement and consider many things:
  - Re-purchase option - cannot be for No consideration or Nominal consideration
  - Looks to see if "lessee" has a Residual Interest in property
  - Looks at the PV of the rental payments to see if it is pretty much equal to price of the property (+ interest under a typical financing arrangement)
  - If Lessee assumes risk or pays insurance or taxes, if he must file, or if he must register the lease.

- **Residual Interests** - Lessor must have a "meaningful" residual interest; If a court finds either of the following factors met, it deems that the Residual Interest belongs to the "lessee," and classifies the transaction as a S/I:
  - If lease gives the property for its entire economic life
  - or • If lessee is bound to renew the lease for the remaining life of the property.
  - or • If lessee has the *option* to renew the lease for the remaining life for no/nominal consideration
  - or • If Lessor <u>credits</u> to the lessee the entire amount of proceeds received upon sale following default

- **Nominal Consideration** -
  In trying to define "Nominal Consideration", courts consider:
  - If it is less than lessee's *reasonably predicted* cost of performing under the lease arrangement
  - If the option price is nominal compared to the value of the property at the end of the lease it is NOT considered nominal if option price is to be determined with FMV at the end of lease
- **Fixtures:** It is very difficult to claim a lease in a fixture. Courts often look to see how much it would costs to remove the fixture from the Real Property.

- When examining the lease, we look at both the "cancelable" and non-cancelable portions, and look to see what remedy "lessor" would get in each situation if the "lessee" defaulted. (Note: One part can be considered a "true lease" while the other can be considered a S/I.)

RELEVANT RULES: 1-201(37)

§1-201(37): The Security Interest:

a) A **"Security Interest"** ("S/I") is:
   1. An interest in personal property or fixtures which *secures payment or performance* of an obligation.

   or 2. Any interest of a buyer of Accounts or Chattel Paper which is subject to Article 9 (under §9-106, §9-105(b), and §9-104(f)).

b) The effect of a *retention* or *reservation* of Title by the seller (in the collateral) is limited to a reservation of a S/I (even if shipped and delivered pursuant to §2-401).

c) The property interest granted in §2-401 (when a seller identifies goods intended for buyer) is not a S/I, *unless* the requirements of Article 9 are met (i.e. attachment and perfection).

d) **Consignment** - the reservation of title in a consignment is not a S/I unless it is *intended* to be a Security Interest (subject to §2-326).

e) **Leases**

1. Look at the facts of each case to determine if a transaction creates a lease or a S/I.

2. A S/I is created if the consideration for the lease is
   i) For the term of the lease (Not subject to termination by the Lessee)
   and ii) *Either:*

   (a) The original term of the lease is ≥ the remaining economic life of the goods.
   or (b) The Lessee is required to *either:*
   1) Renew the lease for the remaining economic life
   or 2) Buy the goods
   or (c) The Lessee has an Option to Renew the lease for the remaining economic life of the goods for *either:*
   1) No Additional Consideration
   or 2) Nominal Consideration
   or (d) The Lessee has the Option to Buy the goods for *either:*
   1) No additional Consideration
   or 2) Nominal Consideration

3. A transaction will <u>not</u> necessarily be considered a S/I if it merely provides that:

(a) The PV of the consideration (rent) is *substantially* ≥ the FMV of the goods at the time of entering into the lease agreement.

or (b) The Lessee:

1. Assume Risk of Loss

or 2. Pays Taxes, Insurance, Filing, Recording, and Registration Fees

or 3. Pays for Service and/or Maintenance of goods

or (c) The Lessee has the option to Renew the lease or Buy goods.

or (d) The Lessee has the option to Renew the lease for a Fixed rent the *reasonably predictable* FMV of rent at the time of the option

or (e) The Lessee has an option to Buy goods for a Fixed Price ≥ the *reasonably predictable* FMV of goods at time of option.

4. <u>**Definitions:**</u>

(x) **"Nominal Consideration"** -

1) <u>Consideration is NOT Nominal if:</u>

(i) The renewal rent is the FMV at the time of the option.

or (ii) The Purchase price is the FMV at the time of the option.

2) <u>Consideration IS Nominal if</u> it is < the lessee's reasonably predicted cost of performing under the lease (if option isn't exercised)

(y) **"Reasonably Predictable"** and **"Remaining Economic Life"** are to be determined with reference to the *<u>facts and circumstances</u>* at the time transaction is entered into.

(z) **"Present Value"** (the amount of future payments discounted to a certain date):

1) The Discount Rate is determined by the interest rate specified by the parties (if reasonable)

2) If there is no rate in agreement, the interest rate = the *<u>Commercially Reasonable Rate</u>* that would be applied in a similar the situation (under the circumstances).

IV. CONSIGNMENTS

1. GENERAL DISTINCTIONS: CONSIGNMENT V. S/I

OVERVIEW

- Like leases, it is important to make the determination as to whether a transaction is a consignment or a S/I for 2 main reasons:
    - Remedy: If a consignment, consignor can repossess collateral - no need to sell it.
    - If it is a consignment, goods are not subject to Debtor's creditors (no need to file).
- Court's consider what type of transaction occurs and determine the interest in the property
    - Sale on Approval - Owned by Consignor; No need to file
    - Sale on Return - Owned by Consignor; Must file pursuant to §9-114
    - S/I - Owned by Consignee; Must File as other Security Interests

- Note: "Sale or Return" (1)(b) vs. (3):
  - Some courts believe that there is a distinction between the "Sale or Return" described in §2-326(1)(b) and the one described in §2-326(3)
  - Effect of Difference: Those interpreting §2-326 to make two different "Sale or Return" categories, have inferred the following differences:
    - Default **with** insolvency (to avoid subjugation to other Creditors):
      - One must file with a §2-326(3) Sale or Return (as per §9-114);
      - Filing does not help under §2-326(1)(b) Sale or Return
    - Default **without** insolvency:
      - One may repossess under §2-326(1)(b)
      - Under §2-326(3) one may only repossess if one filed (as per §9-114)

2. *DEFINITION:*

RELEVANT RULES: 2-326

§2-326: Consignment:

(1) If delivered goods may be Returned by the "Buyer" (even though they conform), the transaction is considered *either:*

(a) A "**Sale on Approval**" - if the goods are delivered primarily for use (ex: trial period)

or (b) A "**Sale or Return**" - if the goods are delivered primarily for resale

(2) Effect of classification:(subject to (3) below)

a) <u>"Sale on Approval"</u> goods are not subject to "buyer's" creditors until goods are **accepted**

b) <u>"Sale or Return"</u> goods are subject to "buyer's" creditors while in the "buyer's" **possession**

(3) <u>"Sale or Return"</u>

i) Goods are deemed to be **<u>"Sale or Return"</u>** if:

a) Goods are delivered to a person for the purpose of resale

and b) The person (consignee) maintains a place of business (where he deals in goods of the kind involved)

and c) The Consignee sells the goods under a name other than the name of the person making the delivery (i.e. the Consignor).

ii) <u>Form over Substance:</u> These provisions apply even if:

a) Title is agreed not to pass until payment or resale

or b) The contract uses words such as "on consignment" or "on memorandum"

iii) <u>EXCEPTIONS to "Sale or Return" Classification</u>:

(a) The person making the delivery complies with an applicable law providing for consignor's interests to be *Evidenced by a Sign.*

or (b) The person making delivery establishes that the person conducting business is known by creditors to be *"substantially engaged in selling the goods of others"* (ex: a known auction house).

or (c) The person making delivery complies with filing provisions of Article 9.

(4) Any "or return" term of a contract for sale is considered

a) A separate contract for sale within the Statute of Frauds (§2-204)

and b) To be contradicting the sale aspect of the contract (within the provisions for parol or extrinsic evidence (as per §2-202))

3. *<u>ATTACHMENT:</u>*

Sales Agreement

4. *PERFECTION:*

May have to file

RELEVANT RULES: 9-114

§9-114: Priority and Filing For Consignments:(see also §2-326):

(1) Priority of Consignors:

i) A person delivering goods under a Consignment which is not a S/I (and required to be filed as per §2-326(3)(c)) has priority over a Secured Pty of the Consignee who:

a) Has a perfected S/I in consignee's goods

and b) Has a S/I in identifiable Cash Proceeds (received on or before delivery of the goods to a buyer)

ii) This rule applies only if

(a) The Consignor **Files** (pursuant to §2-326(3)(c)) *before* the consignee receives possession of the goods.

and (b) Consignor gives **Written Notice** to all holders of a S/I if:

1. The S/I is in the *same type* of goods as those being consigned
2. The Secured Pty filed a F/S before Consignor files (or delivers goods)

and (c) The Secured Pty receives notification within 5 Yrs. before Consignee receives possession of consigned goods.

and (d) The Notification:

1. States that Consignor intends to deliver goods to Consignee on Consignment

and 2. Describes the goods (by item or type)

and e) The Consignment is not considered a S/I

and f) Filing is required (pursuant to §2-326(3)(c))

(2) A person delivering goods to another (i.e. consignor) becomes a *junior* Creditor to a Secured Pty who would have been perfected if:
   a) The goods were property of the Debtor
   and b) *Either:*
      1. The Consignment is not a S/I
      or 2. The above requirements have not been met

5. ***PROCEEDS:***

If A S/I, general proceed rules apply; if a consignment, consignment rules apply.

6. ***PRIORITY:***

If a Consignment, Consignor owns property; If a S/I, must see if it is perfected.

V. CHATTEL PAPER

1. DEFINITION:

§9-105(1)(b): Definitions:

(1) The following definitions apply only to Article 9, unless the context otherwise requires:

* * *

(b) **Chattel Paper -**

1. A Written note, providing for both
   1. A monetary obligation

   and 2. *Either:*
      a) A Security Interest

      or b) A Lease of specific goods
2. Chattel Paper is NOT a Charter or other contract involving the use or hire of a vessel
3. A group of writings taken together will constitute Chattel Paper if a transaction is evidenced by both:
   a) A Security Agreement (or lease)

   and b) An Instrument (or a series of instruments

* * *

2. *GENERAL CHARACTERISTICS:*

- Chattel Paper is like an assignment of a S/I: it is an assignment of the right to payment of another person's S/I (and remaining collateral)

- Parties involved: Buyer --- Account Debtor ---- Creditor

- Types of Chattel Paper Financing:
  - **Notification Financier** - of Chattel Paper, takes POSSESSION of the Chattel Paper and acts as a collecting agency (collects directly from Buyer) Note: MUST give notice to "Buyer"
  - **Non-Notification Financier** - of Chattel Paper, FILES, relies on payment by Account Debtor (no need to give notice to Buyer because they don't deal with Cr), Normally in these transactions, the S/P (bank) *Stamps* the Chattel Paper to put potential possessory parties on Actual Notice of their security.

- It is, therefore, much safer to perfect by possession of the Chattel Paper than to file

- According to §9-308, POSSESSORY Chattel Paper holders take priority over FILED Chattel Paper holders
  - Possessory Chattel Paper holders can take priority of Chattel Paper even after another S/P files -- as long as they don't have Actual Notice of the prior Secured Pty's interest (i.e. no need to check files)
  - Even without Actual Knowledge, the Filer loses to the Possessor when a filer has a claim over the Chattel Paper as proceeds

3. *ATTACHMENT:*

Contract; Security Agreement

4. *PERFECTION:*

Possession or Filing (possession is better)

RELEVANT RULES: §9-304(1); §9-103(4); §9-306(5)

§9-304(1): Perfection Of Instruments:

(1) Perfecting Instruments

a) A S/I in Chattel Paper or Negotiable Documents may be perfected by filing.

b) A S/I in Money or Instruments (other than chattel paper) can only be perfected by **Possession** *unless:*

1) It is an Instrument which is **temporarily perfected** under §9-304(4) or (5)

2) It is Proceeds, which is **temporarily perfected** under §9-306(2) or (3)

§9-103(4): Perfecting Chattel Paper in Multi-State Transactions:

The following rules apply to perfecting Chattel Paper:

a) Possessory S/I - §9-103(1) *"Last Events Test"* applies if the Chattel Paper is in the possession of the S/P

b) Non-Possessory S/I - §9-103(3) applies (file in Debtor's location) if the Chattel Paper is not in the possession of the S/P

c) A S/I in Chattel Paper may not be perfected by notification to the Account Debtor

§9-306(5): Priorities in Proceeds with Returned/Repossessed Goods

i) **Requirements for Priority**:

a) The Sale of goods must result in an Account or Chattel Paper which is transferred by the seller to the S/P.

and b) The goods must be *returned* or *repossessed* by the Debtor or the S/P.

ii) **Rules of Priorities for Returned/Repossessed Goods**

(a) RE-PERFECTION: The Original Security Interest *re-attaches* to the goods, continuing perfection if:

1. The goods were collateral at the time of the sale

and 2. The debt attached to collateral not paid at the sale

and 3. It was perfected when the goods were sold

and 4. *Either:*

a. If **Perfection by Filing:** S/P files a new F/S *only* if the original Filing is not still effective

or b. If **Non-Filed Perfection:** S/P takes possession of goods or file a new F/S

(b) CHATTEL PAPER:

1. An unpaid Transferee of the Chattel Paper maintains a S/I in the goods against the transferor.
2. If Transferee of Chattel Paper is entitled to priority (pursuant to §9-308), then he takes priority over RE-PERFECTED Secured Ptys (see (a)above).

(c) ACCOUNTS:

1. An unpaid Transferee of an account has a S/I in goods against the Transferor.
2. This S/I is *subordinate* to a re-perfected S/I (see (a) above)

(d) A S/I of an unpaid transferee (pursuant to (b) and (c)) must be perfected to protect themselves against

1. Creditors of the Transferor

and 2. Purchasers of the returned/repossessed goods

5. PROCEEDS:

- Proceeds of Chattel Paper:
  - If a S/P has a S/I in Inventory and it becomes a PMSI, which later becomes Chattel Paper, it is best for you to take Possession of the Chattel Paper to insure priority (Note: to maintain perfection he may have to re-file(see §9-306)).
  - Once Chattel Paper becomes proceeds, whoever had priority over the Chattel Paper (before conversion) has priority over the proceeds (thus, if Chattel Paper becomes an A/R or Inventory, the A/R or Inventory Secured Pty will not take priority over the Chattel Paper party if the Chattel Paper party would've has superior priority before the Chattel Paper was converted into proceeds).
  - NOTE: FILING: If a S/P had possession of the Chattel Paper, and it was converted into Inventory or A/R, the S/P must (see §9-306(5)(ii)(d)):
    - File for the Inventory within <u>10 days</u>

    or
    - Take Possession within <u>10 days</u>
  - Some courts say re-filing not necessary -- all that you had superior priority before Chattel Paper was converted

6. PRIORITY:

Possession is superior to filing

RELEVANT RULE: §9-308

§9-308: Chattel Paper and Instruments:

Purchasers of Chattel Paper or Instruments take Priority over a S/I in that Chattel Paper or Instrument if the purchaser takes it:

(a) **Without Knowledge of S/I**: To maintain priority, the Purchaser must prove that:

1. Purchaser took *without knowledge* that the Chattel Paper or Instrument is subject to a S/I

and 2. New Value was given for it

and 3. He took Possession of the Chattel Paper in the Ordinary Course of his Business

and 4. It is Perfected under *either:*

a) §9-304 (permissive filing and temporary perfection)

or b) §9-306 (perfection as to proceeds)

or (b) **With Knowledge**: To maintain priority, the Purchaser must prove that:

1. The Instrument or Chattel Paper is *Proceeds of Inventory*, subject to a S/I (as per §9-306) even though he knows that the specific Chattel Paper or Instrument. is subject to a S/I

and 2. New Value was given for it

and 3. He took Possession of the Chattel Paper in the *Ordinary Course of his Business*

7. CHATTEL PAPER *TRANSACTIONS NOT COVERED BY ARTICLE 9:*

§9-104(f): Transactions Excluded From Article 9:

Article 9 does not apply to the **Sale of Accounts or Chattel Paper** if:

1. They are part of a Sale of the Business from which they originated

or 2. They are an *Assignment* for the purpose of Collection ONLY

or 3. They are a Transfer of a Right to Payment to an Assignee who is also obligated to perform under the contract

or 4. They are a transfer of a Single Account to an Assignee in satisfaction (in whole or in part) of a preexisting debt

VI. FIXTURES

1. DEFINITION:

§9-313: Priority In Fixtures:

(1) **General Definitions**

(a) Goods are **"Fixtures"** when they become so related to *particular* Real Estate that an interest in them arises under Real Estate Law.

(b) A **"Fixture Filing"** is a filing of a financing statement for fixture goods in the office where Real Estate mortgages are filed or recorded (pursuant to §9-402(5)).

(c) A **"Constructive Mortgage"** is a mortgage that secures an obligation incurred for the *construction of an improvement* on the land (If the recorded writing indicates, the Constructive mortgage may include the cost to acquire the land).

(2) **Security Interests in Fixtures:**

a) A Security Interest in Fixtures:

1. May be created in goods which are fixtures

and 2. May *continue* in goods which become fixtures

b) A S/I may not be created (under Article 9) in ordinary building materials incorporated into an improvement on land.

(3) This Article does not prevent the creation of a fixture lien ("encumbrance") pursuant to the state's Real Estate law

(4) **Priority of a Perfected Fixture S/I:** A Perfected S/I in fixtures has *priority* over a conflicting interest of the Owner or a lien-holder of the Real Property ("Encumbrancer") only if the Fixture S/I is:

(a) **A PMSI** only if:
1. The goods become fixtures *after* the Owner's or the Encumbrancer's interest arises

and 2. The S/I is perfected by **Fixture Filing**
a) Before the goods became fixtures
or b) Within 10 Days after they became fixtures

and 3. The Debtor has
a) Possession of the Real Estate
or b) A Recorded interest in the Real Estate

or (b) **Filed First** only if:
1. The S/I was perfected by Fixture Filing *before* the Owner or Encumbrancer recorded their interests

and 2. The S/I has priority over any conflicting interest of a predecessor in the Owner or Encumbrancer's title

and 3. The Debtor has
a) Possession of the Real Estate
or b) A Recorded interest in the Real Estate

or (c) **In Removable Fixtures** only if:
1. The fixtures are:
a) Readily removable factory or office machines
or b) Readily removable replacements of Domestic Appliances (which are consumer goods)

and 2. The S/I was perfected *before* the goods became fixtures (by any method allowed by this Article)

or (d) **A Judicial Lien** only if the conflicting interest is a judicial lien on the Real Estate, obtained *after* the S/I was perfected (by any method allowed by this Article (ex: judgment obtained in a court of law))

(5) **Priority of an Unperfected Fixture S/I:** A S/I in fixtures, *whether or not perfected*, has Priority over a conflicting Owner or Encumbrancer of Real Estate if:

(a) The Owner or Encumbrancer has
1. Consented in writing to the S/I
or 2. Disclaimed an interest in the goods as fixtures

or (b) The Debtor has a right to remove the goods as against the Owner or Encumbrancer.
(Note: If the Debtor loses this right, the priority of the S/I continues for a "reasonable time").

(6) **Priority against Construction Mortgages:**
a) A S/I in fixtures is Subordinate to a **Construction Mortgage** if:
1. The Construction Mortgage was recorded *before* the goods became Fixtures
and 2. The goods became fixtures *before* the completion of the construction

b) If a Mortgage is given to refinance a Construction Mortgage it has the same priority as the Construction Mortgage.

c) This section is subject to (4) and (5) above, but not subsection (4)(a) for PMSI Fixtures.

(7) **All Other Cases:**
a) In all other cases not within the preceding subsections, a S/I in Fixtures is Subordinate to the Owner's or Encumbrancer's conflicting interest in the fixtures.
b) This rule (9-313(7)) only applies if the Owner or Encumbrancer is NOT the Debtor.

(8) **Removal of Collateral Upon Default**

a) If a S/P has priority over all Owners and Encumbrancers, he may remove his collateral from the Real Estate if the Debtor defaults (subject to Part 5).

b) **Reimbursement:**

1. The S/P Must *reimburse* any Encumbrancer or Owner of the Real Estate for the cost to repair any *physical injury* resulting from the removal if:
   a The Owner or Encumbrancer is not the Debtor
   or b. The Owner or Encumbrancer has not otherwise greed

2. The S/P need NOT Reimburse the Owner or Encumbrancer for:
   a. Any loss in value of the Real Estate cause by the absence of the removed goods
   or b. The loss incurred by any necessity of *replacing* the goods

3. Those parties entitled to reimbursement may *refuse* permission for the S/P to remove his collateral until he gives them *adequate security* that he will reimburse them for the appropriate damages.

2. *ATTACHMENT:*

Security Agreement

3. PERFECTION:

RELEVANT RULES: §9-401(1); §9-401(5); §9-402(5); §9-402(6); §9-403(6)

§9-401(1): Place Of Filing For Fixtures(INTRASTATE):

The proper place, within a state, to file in order to perfect a S/I in goods which are or will become fixtures:

ALTERNATIVE I

(a) Office where Real Estate Mortgage would be filed

* * *

ALTERNATIVE II

* * *

(b) Office where Real Estate Mortgage would be filed

ALTERNATIVE III

* * *

(b) Office where Real Estate Mortgage would be filed

* * *

§9-401(5): Filing Transmitting Utilities and Fixture Filing:

a) The proper place for filing a Fixture or Transmitting Utility is the Secretary of State.

b) This section is Subject to §9-302(3)

c) This section supersedes any previous sections above (i.e. §9-401)

§9-402(5): Financing Statements For Fixtures:

1) Financing Statements must describe Real Estate for collateral of

a) Natural Resources (oil, gas, minerals, timber)

b) Accounts subject to §9-103(5)

c) Fixture Financing Statement (as per §9-313) for goods which are (or will become) fixtures

2) F/S Requirements:

a) Show that it covers this type of collateral

and b) Recite that it is filed in the Real Estate records

and c) Give enough detail of the Real Property -sufficient to give Constructive Notice of the mortgage or Real Property (pursuant to the state law)

3) If the Debtor does not have an interest of record in the land then F/S must show the name of a "record owner" (of the property)

§9-402(6) Fixture Filing Mortgages:

i) A Mortgage is effective as a F/S for Fixture Filings from the date of its recording if:

(a) The goods are described in the mortgage by item or type

and (b) The goods are to become (or already are) fixtures related to the Real Estate described in the mortgage

and (c) The mortgage complies with this section's requirements for a F/S (except that it need not state that it is to be filed in the Real Estate office)

and (d) The mortgage is duly recorded

ii) A fee for filing the F/S is not required; only the regular recording and satisfaction fees with respect to the mortgage are required.

§9-403(6): Expiration of a Fixture Filing

* * *

A Mortgage filed as a Fixture Filing (as per §9-402(6)) is effective until:

1. The mortgage is released or satisfied

or 2. Its effectiveness otherwise terminates as to the real estate

3. *ASSIGNMENT*

§9-405(2): Assignment Of Fixtures:

Statement of Assignment:

a. A S/P may assign - *on the record* - all or part of his rights under a F/S by filing a Separate Written **Statement of Assignment**

b. The Statement of Assignment must

1. Be in Writing

and 2. Be signed by the Secured Pty of Record

and 3. Set forth the Name of the Debtor and Secured Pty of Record

and 4. Include the File # and Date that original F/S was filed

and 5. Contain the Name and Address of the Assignee

and 6. Describe the collateral assigned

c. A Copy of the Assignment may be used if it contains the required information (as stated above).

d. Upon presentation of the Statement of Assignment, the Filing Officer shall:

1. Mark the Statement with the date and hour of filing
2. Note the Statement of Assignment on the Index *either:*
   a) Under the Name of the Assignor (as Grantor) - for Assignments of
      1) Fixture filings
      2) Filing covering timber to be cut
      3) Minerals (or the like)
      4) Accounts subject to §9-103(5) (filing where Debtor lives)

   *** Note: Must also index the Financing Statement under the name of the Assignee if the state requires filing assignments of mortgages under the assignee's name

   or b) Under the Financing Statement - for all other filings

3. An Assignment of Record - for a S/I in a Fixture (perfected by including the fixture on a mortgage filing (see §9-402(6)) may only be made by assigning the Mortgage (as provided by the law of the State)

4. Fee Schedule * * *

VII. ASSIGNMENTS

1. FILING:

RELEVANT RULES:§9-405; §9-302(1)

§9-405: Assignment Of Security Interest:

(1) **Assignment on the Financing Statement**

a. An Assignment of a Security Interest may be disclosed by

1. Indicating the *Name* and *Address* of the Assignee on the F/S

or 2. By attaching a copy on the face or the back of the F/S

b. The Filing Officer shall mark the F/S upon presentation (pursuant to §9-403(4))

c. Fee Schedule * * *

(2) **Statement of Assignment**:

a. A S/P may assign - *on the record* - all or part of his rights under a F/S by filing a Separate Written **Statement of Assignment**

b. The Statement of Assignment must

1. Be in Writing

and 2. Be signed by the Secured Pty of Record

and 3. Set forth the Name of the Debtor and Secured Pty of Record

and 4. Include the File # and Date that original F/S was filed

and 5. Contain the Name and Address of the Assignee

and 6. Describe the collateral assigned

c. A Copy of the Assignment may be used if it contains the required information (as stated above).

d. Upon presentation of the Statement of Assignment, the Filing Officer shall:

1. Mark the Statement with the date and hour of filing
2. Note the Statement of Assignment on the Index *either:*

a) Under the Name of the Assignor (as Grantor) - for Assignments of

1) Fixture filings
2) Filing covering timber to be cut
3) Minerals (or the like)
4) Accounts subject to §9-103(5) (filing where Debtor lives)

*** Note: Must also index the Financing Statement under the name of the Assignee if the state requires filing assignments of mortgages under the assignee's name

or b) Under the Financing Statement - for all other filings

3. An Assignment of Record - for a S/I in a Fixture (perfected by including the fixture on a mortgage filing (see §9-402(6)) may only be made by assigning the Mortgage (as provided by the law of the State)

4. Fee Schedule * * *

(3) The Assignee will become the "Secured Pty of Record" after disclosure or filing of an assignment under this section.

§9-302(1)(e),(g): Filing Is Not Required for Assignments:

* * *

The following Assignments do not have to be flied for perfection:

(e) An **Assignment of Accounts,** which does not transfer a significant part of the assignor's accounts (alone or in conjunction with other assignments to the same Assignee)

* * *

or (g) **An Assignment:**

1. For the benefit of all creditors of the transferor

and 2. Subsequent transfers by the Assignee

2. *SET-OFFS & DEFENSES:*

- If a S/I is assigned, the Debtor has a right to "set-off" the obligation with any "defenses" he has against the original Creditor *so long as* the "defenses" have accrued by the time Debtor pays his debt or has the collateral disposed of (i.e. if Cr owed Debtor money, due on Day 5, Debtor cannot assert defense against Assignee until Day 5) (this often happens when seller (PMSI Creditor) factors debt to a bank).
- This also occurs if the Assignor is the original Creditor. Debtor may "set-off" obligation to the original Creditor if he has a defense against the seller (i.e. goods are no good; deducting $1,000 for deficiency)
- The Assignee will, thus, get less than he expected, he may sue the Creditor (assignor) for the balance
- §9-318(3) protects a Debtor from paying a Seller who has his debt to a new Creditor. The Debtor is not obligated to pay the new Creditor until he received notice that debt is now owed to new Creditor

- If Debtor is insolvent, however, he may not "set-off" he must pay Creditor the entire debt, and sue the seller for any "defense"

RELEVANT RULES:§9-206; §9-318

§9-206: Agreement Not To Assert Defenses Against Assignee:

(1) Creating an Agreement Not to Assert Defenses Against Assignee:

a) An agreement by a Buyer (or Lessee) not to assert a Claim or Defense against an Assignee (which it may have against the Assignor of the Security Interest (seller/lessor)) is Enforceable if

1. The Assignee takes the assignment:

a. In Good Faith

and b. Paid Value for the assignment

and c. Without Notice of a Claim or Defense

and 2. The claim is not one which could be asserted against a Holder-In-Due Course (HDC) of a Negotiable Instrument (under Article 3)

b) A Buyer who signs *both* a Negotiable Instrument and a Security Agreement as part of *one* transaction makes an Agreement not to Assert Defenses Against an Assignee

c) This rule is subject to any statute/decision which establishes a different rule for buyers or lessees of consumer goods.

(2) Modification of Sales Warranties where Security Agreement Exists:

When a seller sells a PMSI in goods, Article 2 governs the sale and any disclaimer, limitation, or modification of the seller's warranties.

§9-318: Assignments:

(1) Defenses Against Assignees: Unless the Account Debtor has made an enforceable agreement not to assert Defenses or Claims arising out of a sale (as per §9-206), the rights of an Assignee are subject to:

(a) **Contractual Terms:** All Terms of the Contract between the Account Debtor and Assignor, *including* any Claim or Defense arising from the contract

(b) **"Set Offs"** (outside contact): Any other defense or claim that the Account Debtor has against the Assignor, as long as it accrues *before* the Account Debtor received notification of the assignment.

(2) Modification of Contract After Notification of Assignment

a. Any Modification of or Substitution for the Contract will be effective against the Assignee, *whether or not notification of assignment has been given,* if:

1. It is made in Good Faith

and 2. It is in accordance with *Reasonable Commercial Standards*

and 3. The Right to Payment has not been fully earned by performance under the assigned contract

and 4. The Account Debtor has not otherwise agreed

b. The Assignee acquires the Assignor's corresponding rights under the Modified or Substituted Contract.

c. The Assignment may provide that such a Modification or Substitution is a breach by the Assignor if a Perfected S/I is assigned.

(3) Identification and Proof of Assignment

a. The Account Debtor is Authorized to pay the *Assignor* until the Account Debtor receives notice that:

1. An assignment has been made

and 2. That payment shall be made to the Assignee

b. A Notification which does not *reasonably identify* the rights assigned to the Assignee is *ineffective*

c. The Account Debtor may continue to pay the Assignor until the Assignee provides *reasonable proof* (upon Debtor's request) that the assignment has actually been made.

(4) <u>Term Prohibiting Assignment Ineffective</u>: A Term in any contract between an Account Debtor and an Assignor is *ineffective* if it:

a. Prohibits the Assignment of an account

or b. Prohibits the creation of a S/I in a general intangible for money due or to become due

or c. Requires the Account Debtor's consent for such assignment or S/I

THE

E-Z RULES

FOR

ARTICLE 9

E-Z RULES TABLE OF CONTENTS

RELEVANT DEFINITIONS

ARTICLE 9

PART I SHORT TITLE, APPLICABILITY AND DEFINITIONS

PART 2 VALIDITY OF THE SECURITY AGREEMENT AND THE RIGHTS OF THE PARTIES

PART 3: PRIORITIES AND RIGHTS OF PARTIES

SELECTED BANKRUPTCY STATUTES

RELEVANT DEFINITIONS

The Following Definitions Apply to the Entire UCC, Including Article 9:

§1-201(9): Buyer In The Ordinary Course Of Business:

1. A "Buyer In The Ordinary Course" ("BIOC") is an Individual/Organization (not a pawnbroker) who buys goods:
   - a) In Good Faith (see §1-201(19))
   - and b) Without knowledge that purchase is in violation of someone else's S/I (or other ownership rights)
   - and c) From a 'Merchant' - someone in the business of selling *those* goods (except a pawnbroker)
   - and d) In the *Ordinary Course* - passing of title *for value* (i.e. a sale) in a typical transaction (ex: inventory, not equipment)
   - and e) For **Value**

2. Anyone selling minerals, oil, or gas (at wellhead or minehead) is considered to be in the business of selling goods of that kind.

3. How Goods May Be Bought:
   - a) For Cash
   - or b) By Exchange of property
   - or c) On Credit - secured or unsecured
   - or d) Receiving goods/title under a pre-existing contract for sale

4. Goods are NOT considered Bought if:
   - a) They are given as a security for a debt
   - b) They are given as partial or total satisfaction of a debt
   - c) They are transferred in bulk

§1-201(19): Good Faith:

"Good Faith" means Honesty in Fact in the Conduct or Transaction Concerned.

§1-203: Good Faith:

"Every contract or duty within this Act imposes an obligation of Good Faith in its performance or enforcement"(see §1-201(19)).

§1-201(30): Person:

A Person includes an individual or organization.

§1-201(37): The Security Interest:

a) A **"Security Interest"** ("S/I") is:
   1. An interest in personal property or fixtures which *secures payment or performance* of an obligation.
   or 2. Any interest of a buyer of Accounts or Chattel Paper which is subject to Article 9 (under §9-106, §9-105(b), and §9-104(f)).

b) The effect of a *retention* or *reservation* of Title by the seller (in the collateral) is limited to a reservation of a S/I (even if shipped and delivered pursuant to §2-401).

c) The property interest granted in §2-401 (when a seller identifies goods intended for buyer) is not a S/I, *unless* the requirements of Article 9 are met (i.e. attachment and perfection).

d) **Consignment** - the reservation of title in a consignment is not a S/I unless it is *intended* to be a Security Interest (subject to §2-326).

e) **Leases**

1. Look at the <u>facts of each case</u> to determine if a transaction creates a lease or a S/I.

2. A S/I is created if the consideration for the lease is
   i) <u>For the term of the lease</u> (Not subject to termination by the Lessee)
   and ii) *<u>Either:</u>*

   (a) The original term of the lease is >= the remaining economic life of the goods.
   or (b) The Lessee is <u>required</u> to *either:*
      1) Renew the lease for the remaining economic life
      or 2) Buy the goods
   or (c) The Lessee has an <u>Option to Renew</u> the lease for the remaining economic life of the goods for *either:*
      1) No Additional Consideration
      or 2) Nominal Consideration
   or (d) The Lessee has the <u>Option to Buy</u> the goods for *either:*
      1) No additional Consideration
      or 2) Nominal Consideration

3. A transaction will <u>not</u> necessarily be considered a S/I if it merely provides that:
   (a) The PV of the consideration (rent) is *substantially* >= the FMV of the goods at the time of entering into the lease agreement.
   or (b) The Lessee:
      1. Assume Risk of Loss
      or 2. Pays Taxes, Insurance, Filing, Recording, and Registration Fees
      or 3. Pays for Service and/or Maintenance of goods
   or (c) The Lessee has the option to Renew the lease or Buy goods.
   or (d) The Lessee has the option to Renew the lease for a Fixed rent the *reasonably predictable* FMV of rent at the time of the option
   or (e) The Lessee has an option to Buy goods for a Fixed Price >= the *reasonably predictable* FMV of goods at time of option.

4. **Definitions:**

(x) **"Nominal Consideration"** -

1) Consideration is NOT Nominal if:

(i) The renewal rent is the FMV at the time of the option.

or (ii) The Purchase price is the FMV at the time of the option.

2) Consideration IS Nominal if it is < the lessee's reasonably predicted cost of performing under the lease (if option isn't exercised)

(y) **"Reasonably Predictable"** and **"Remaining Economic Life"** are to be determined with reference to the *facts and circumstances* at the time transaction is entered into.

(z) **"Present Value"** (the amount of future payments discounted to a certain date):

1) The Discount Rate is determined by the interest rate specified by the parties (if reasonable)

2) If there is no rate in agreement, the interest rate = the *Commercially Reasonable Rate* that would be applied in a similar the situation (under the circumstances).

§1-201(44): Value:

1) A Person is deemed to give **"Value"** if he acquires his rights *either:*

(a) In return for *either:*

1. A Binding Commitment to **Extend Credit** (ex: L/C)

or 2. An Extension of **Immediately Available Credit**

or (b) A Security for total or partial **satisfaction** of a pre-existing claim

or (c) By accepting delivery pursuant to a pre-existing contract for purchase

or (d) In return for any "sufficient" consideration (as would support a simple contract)

2) This section is subject to:

a) §3-303: Negotiable Instruments

b) §4-208; §4-209: Bank Collections

PART 1:

SCOPE OF ARTICLE 9

§9-101: Short Title:

"This Article shall be known and may be cited as Uniform Commercial Code - Secured Transactions."

§9-102: Policy & Subject Of Article 9:

(1) Except as provided in §9-104, Article 9 applies to:

(a) Any transaction *intended to create a Security Interest* (regardless of form) in Personal Property or Fixtures, including:

1. Goods
or 2. Documents
or 3. Instruments
or 4. General Intangibles
or 5. Chattel paper
or 6. Accounts

and (b) Any sale of Accounts or Chattel Paper

(2) Article 9 also applies to <u>Security Interests made by Contract,</u> including:

a. Pledges
and b. Assignments
and c. Chattel Mortgages/Trusts
and d. Conditional Sales
and e. Trust Receipts
and f. Factor's Liens
and g. Trust Deeds
and h. Equipment Trusts
and i. Liens (NOT Statutory liens, unless provided for in §9-310)
and j. Title Retention Contracts
and k. Leases or Consignments <u>Intended as a Security Interest</u>
(see §1-201(37))

(3) The application of this Article is not affected by the fact that an obligation is secured by a transaction or interest which this Article does not apply to.

§9-103: Perfecting Multi-State Transactions:

(1) **Documents, Instruments, Letters of Credit and Ordinary Goods:** (i.e. Collateral must have a definite location)

(a) This section does not apply to:

1) Certificates of Title (as per §9-103(2))

or 2) Mobile Goods (as per §9-103(3))

or 3) Minerals (as per §9-103(5))

(b) **"Last Events Test":** Rules of Perfection are governed by the laws of the Jurisdiction where the **last** event that is claimed to perfect (or "unperfect") the collateral occurs (a.k.a. "ALL EVENTS TEST").

(c) **PMSI Exception:** If parties creating a PMSI **understand**, *at the time the S/I attaches*, that the goods will be kept in another jurisdiction (i.e. the "proposed jurisdiction"), then the law of the jurisdiction where goods are to be taken applies:

1) Proposed Jurisdiction's laws apply from the time attachment occurs.

2) If goods are actually taken to their proposed jurisdiction, those laws remain in effect.

3) If the goods do not end up in their proposed jurisdiction then the proposed jurisdiction's laws apply for 30 Days from the date of **possession by Debtor**.

(d) **Removal of Collateral:**

1) If collateral is removed from a state where it is subject to the laws of its jurisdiction, the S/I remains perfected.

2) If "Action" to perfect a S/I is required (ex: State requires this type of collateral to be filed), then:

(i) The S/I becomes Unperfected (against Purchasers of the collateral after removal) if the "Action" is not taken before the *earlier of:*

a) The Expiration period of the original jurisdiction's filing

or b) 4 Months after the collateral is brought into the new state

(ii) The S/I Continues to be Perfected if the "Action" is taken before the *earlier of:*

a) The expiration period of the original jurisdiction's filing

or b) 4 Months after the collateral is brought into the new state

(iii) Priority over a BIOC of Consumer Goods (as per §9-307(2)) for collateral which has been removed from its original jurisdiction, has the same "Action" requirements as above ((i), (ii)).

(2) **Certificate of Title**

(Note: This section only applies to goods subject to Certificate of Title statutes; Motor Vehicles generally are not subject to such statutes until they are sold to a purchaser; thus, a new motor vehicle in possession of a retail dealer will probably be subject to (1) or, if the Motor Vehicle is to be leased, subject to (3))

(a) This section applies to goods which require a Certificate of Title (on which a S/I is required to be indicated upon (in order to perfect)).

(b) The law of the jurisdiction **issuing the certificate** governs until:

1) The Certificate is Surrendered

or 2) The *Later of:*

a) 4 Months after removal of the goods from the original jurisdiction

or b) The goods are registered in another jurisdiction

(*** Note: After expiration of the above period, goods are not covered by the Certificate Title within the meaning of this section)

(c) Goods not subject to a Certificate of Title statute in their original jurisdiction are subject to §9-103(d) if they are moved to a jurisdiction requiring a Certificate of Title (unless bought by a Buyer - as discussed in (d) below)

(d) Exception to 4 Month Rule:

If Perfected goods are brought into a new state, and the new state issues a Certificate of Title, *not showing the S/I,* the S/I becomes **Subordinate** to the rights of a Buyer who:

1) Is not a "Merchant" - Isn't in the business of selling the goods

and 2) Gives value

and 3) Receives delivery

and 4) Is Without Knowledge of the S/I

(3) **Accounts, General Intangibles, and Mobile Goods** (Not inventory which isn't leased!):

(a) This section applies to the following if it is not subject to a Certificate of Title statute (as per §9-103(2)):

1) **Accounts** and **General Intangibles** other than uncertified securities

and 2) **Mobile Goods** - Mobile Goods have the following Characteristics:

a) Goods of the type which are normally used in more than one jurisdiction (ex: cars, airplanes)

and b) They are Mobile

and c) They are *either:*

1. **Equipment** - expected to be moved or which have no definite location.

or 2. **Inventory** - to be LEASED by the Debtor to others (see §9-109:Mobile Goods)

(b) The laws of the jurisdiction where the **Debtor is located** governs (laws of perfection, non-perfection, and its effects)

(c) Foreign jurisdiction:

1) The law of the jurisdiction of debtor's main executive office in the U.S. applies if:

a) The Debtor is located outside the USA

and b) The Foreign country does not provide for filing/recording for perfection

2) S/I may be perfected by notifying the Account Debtor if

a) The Debtor is located outside the USA or Canada

and b) The Collateral is Accounts or General Intangibles

(d) **Debtor's Location:**

1) Place of business - under normal circumstances

2) Chief executive office -if more than one place of business

3) Residence -if no place of business

4) Location of designated agent for Service of Process - if a foreign air carrier

(e) **Debtor Changes Location**

1) Perfection made in the place of debtor's location lasts until the earlier of:

a) 4 Months after Debtor moves

or b) Expiration of the original filing - when perfection would have ceased by the law of the first jurisdiction

2) If perfection is not made in the new jurisdiction before the expiration of the above period, then the security becomes unperfected, and is deemed *unperfected* as to a Purchaser of the collateral (after the change of location).

(4) **Chattel Paper**

a) Possessory S/I - §9-103(1) *"Last Events Test"* applies if the Chattel Paper is in the possession of the S/P

b) Non-Possessory S/I - §9-103(3) applies (file in Debtor's location) if the Chattel Paper is not in the possession of the S/P

c) A S/I in Chattel Paper may not be perfected by notification to the Account Debtor.

(5) **Minerals**

The law of the jurisdiction where the **minerals came from** governs perfection when the mineral attaches *either:*

a) As it is exacted

or b) To an account resulting from the sale of the minerals (at the wellhead or minehead)

(6) **Investment Property**

(a) This subsection applies to investment property; it lists the choice of law rules for perfection of security interests in investment property:

(b) **Certificated Security:** During the time that a security certificate is located in a jurisdiction, the following are governed by *the local law of the jurisdiction where the certificate is located* (except as otherwise provided in paragraph (f)):

1. Perfection of a security interest in a certificated security

and 2. The effect of perfection or non-perfection of the security interest

and 3. The priority of the security interest

(c) **Uncertificated Security:** The following are governed by *the local law of the issuer's jurisdiction as specified in Section 8-110(d)* (except as otherwise provided in paragraph (f)):

1. Perfection of a security interest in an uncertificated security

and 2. The effect of perfection or non-perfection of the security interest

and 3. The priority of the security interest

(d) **Security Entitlements/Securities Accounts:** The following are governed by *the local law of the securities intermediary's jurisdiction as specified in Section 8-110(e)* (except as otherwise provided in paragraph (f)):

1. Perfection of a security interest in a security entitlement or securities account

and 2. The effect of perfection or non-perfection of the security interest

and 3. The priority of the security interest

(e) **Commodity Contracts/Commodity Accounts:**

a. The following are governed by *the local law of the commodity intermediary's jurisdiction* (except as otherwise provided in paragraph (f)):

1. Perfection of a security interest in a commodity contract or commodity account

and 2. The effect of perfection or non-perfection of the security interest

and 3. The priority of the security interest

b. The following rules determine what "**commodity intermediary's jurisdiction**" means for purposes of this paragraph:

(i) **Jurisdiction Specified in Agreement:** The "commodity intermediary's jurisdiction" will be the jurisdiction specified in an agreement, if the agreement between the commodity intermediary and commodity customer specifies that it is governed by the law of a particular jurisdiction.

(ii) **Office of Commodity Account Specified in Agreement:** The "commodity intermediary's jurisdiction" will be the jurisdiction specified in an agreement, if:

1. The agreement between the commodity intermediary and commodity customer does not specify the governing law as provided in subparagraph (i).

but 2. It expressly specifies that the commodity account is maintained at an office in a particular jurisdiction.

(iii) **Location Not Specified in Agreement:** The "commodity intermediary's jurisdiction" will be the jurisdiction in which the office identified (in an account statement) as the office serving the commodity customer's account is located, if the agreement between the commodity intermediary and commodity customer does not specify a jurisdiction as provided in subparagraphs (i) or (ii).

(iv) **Location Not Specified and Office Not Identified:** The "commodity intermediary's jurisdiction" will be the jurisdiction in which the chief executive office of the commodity intermediary is located, if:

1. The agreement between the commodity intermediary and commodity customer does not specify a jurisdiction as provided in subparagraphs (i) or (ii).

and 2. An account statement does not identify an office serving the commodity customer's account as provided in subparagraph (iii).

(f) The following are governed by *the local law of the jurisdiction in which the debtor is located:*

1. Perfection of a security interest by filing
2. Automatic perfection of a security interest in **investment property** granted by a broker or securities intermediary
3. Automatic perfection of a security interest in a **commodity contract** or **commodity account** granted by a commodity intermediary

§9-104: Transactions Excluded From Article 9:

This Article does NOT apply to:

(a) A S/I subject to any **U.S. Statute** governing the rights of parties (including Third Pty) affected by transactions in particular types of property.

(b) To a **Landlord's Lien**

(c) To a **Statutory Lien** or Lien for services or materials (unless allowed under §9-310)

(d) To a **Transfer of a Claim for Employee Compensation** (including wages and salary)

(e) To a **Transfer by a Government** or government agency

(f) To the **Sale of Accounts or Chattel Paper** if:
1. They are part of a Sale of the Business from which they originated
or 2. They are an *Assignment* for the purpose of Collection ONLY
or 3. They are a Transfer of a Right to Payment to an Assignee who is also obligated to perform under the contract
or 4. They are a transfer of a Single Account to an Assignee in satisfaction (in whole or in part) of a preexisting debt

(g) To a **Transfer of an Interest in an Insurance Policy**, unless provided for in:
1. §9-306 (Insurance is a Proceed)
and 2. §9-312 (Priorities in Proceeds)

(h) To a **Right represented by a judgment** (unless judgment is on collateral)

(i) Any **Right of Set-off**

(j) **Real Estate Transactions** including:
1. The Creation of an Lien or interest in Real Estate
2. The Transfer of an Lien or interest in Real Estate
3. Any leases or rents thereunder

(k) To a **Transfer of any Tort Claim**

(l) A **Transfer of interest in a Deposit Account** (as per §9-105(1)) unless they are proceeds and provided for in:
1. §9-306 (general proceeds rules)
or 2. §9-312 (priority in proceeds)

(m) A **Transfer of an interest in a Letter of Credit** - other than the rights to proceeds under a written Letter of credit.

§9-105: Definitions:

(1) The following definitions apply only to Article 9, unless the context otherwise requires:

(a) **Account Debtor** - A person who is obligated on an Account, Chattel Paper, or General Intangible.

(b) **Chattel Paper** -
1. A Written note, providing for both
a. A monetary obligation
and b. *Either:*
1) A Security Interest
or 2) A Lease of specific goods
2. Chattel Paper is NOT a Charter or other contract involving the use or hire of a vessel
3. A group of writings taken together will constitute Chattel Paper if a transaction is evidenced by both:
a) A Security Agreement (or lease)
and b) An Instrument (or a series of instruments)

(c) **Collateral** - property subject to a S/I (including Accounts and Chattel Paper which have been sold)

(d) **Debtor** -

1. A person who owes payment/performance of a secured obligation
2. Includes the seller of Chattel Paper or Accounts
3. Debtor need not own or have rights in the collateral
4. If the Debtor is not the owner of the collateral, then:
    a) "**Debtor**" refers to the owner of collateral (in Article 9 provisions dealing w/ collateral)
    b) "**Obligor**" refers to the one owing the debt/obligation (in Article 9 provisions dealing w/ collateral)

(e) **Deposit Account** - a liquid Bank account (not a CD account) (this includes a demand, time, savings, passbook, or like account maintained with a bank, saving and loan association, credit union, or like organization).

(f) **Document** - Document of title

(g) **Encumbrance** - includes Mortgages and other Liens on Real Estate, and all other rights in Real Estate that are not ownership interests.

(h) **Goods** -

1. All things movable at the time the S/I attaches (or fixtures).
2. The following items are NOT Goods:
    a) Money
    or b) Documents
    or c) Instruments
    or d) Accounts
    or e) Chattel Paper
    or f) Minerals before exaction
    or g) General Intangibles
    or h) Investment Property

3. The following items are considered goods
    a) Standing timber (which is to be cut and removed under a contract of sale or conveyance)
    b) Growing Crops
    c) Unborn Animals intended for sale

(i) **Instrument -**

1. The following items are considered Instruments
    a) A Negotiable Instrument (see §3-104)
    b) Investment Property (see §8-102)
    c) Any other writing evidencing a right to the payment of money
2. An Instrument cannot, in itself, be a Security Agreement or lease
3. Instruments may be Transferable by delivery (w/ any necessary endorsements) in the Ordinary Course of business.

(j) **Mortgage** - a Consensual interest created by a Real Estate mortgage or a trust deed.

(k) **Advances made "Pursuant to Commitment"** - Created if the Secured Pty has bound himself to make it, *whether or not* a subsequent event of default (or other event not within his control) has relieved (or may relieve) him from his obligation.

(l) **Security Agreement** - an agreement creating or providing for a security interest.

(m) **Secured Party** - The following entities are considered Secured Parties:

1. A Lender, Seller, or other person in whose favor there is a security interest
2. Buyers of chattel paper and accounts
3. Representatives for "Holders of Obligations" (issued under an Indentured Trust, Equipment Trust agreement, or the like) if they are represented by a trustee or other person.

(o) **Transmitting Utility** - An entity primarily engaged in railroad, bus, electronic communications, transmission of goods by pipeline, production and transmission of electricity, steam, gas, or water, sewer services, or other utilities.

(2) Other definitions applying to this Article:

a. "Account" (§9-106)
b. "Attach" (§9-203)
c. "Commodity Contract" (9-115)
d. "Commodity Customer" (9-115)
e. "Commodity Intermediary" (9-115)
f. "Construction Mortgage" (§9-313(1))
g. "Consumer Goods" (§9-109(1))
h. "Control" (9-115)
i. "Equipment" (§9-109(2))
j. "Farm Products" (§9-109(3))
k. "Fixture" (§9-313(1))
l. "Fixture Filing" (§9-313(1))
m. "General Intangibles" (§9-106)
n. "Inventory" (§9-109(4))
o. "Investment Property" (9-115)
p. "Lien Creditor" (§9-301(3))
q. "Proceeds" (§9-306(1))
r. "Purchase Money Security Interest" (§9-107)
s. "United States" (§9-103)

(3) The following definitions in other Articles apply to this Article:

a. "Broker" (8-102)
b. "Certificated Security" (8-102)
c. "Check" (§3-104)
d. "Clearing Corporation" (8-102)
e. "Contract for Sale" (§2-106)
f. "Control" (8-106)
g. "Delivery" (8-301)
h. "Entitlement Holder" (8-102)
i. "Financial Asset" (8-102)
j. "Holder in Due Course" (§3-302)
k. "Letter of Credit" (§5-102)
l. "Note" (§3-104)
m. "Proceeds of a Letter of Credit" (§5-114(a))
n. "Sale" (§2-106)
o. "Securities Intermediary" (8-102)
p. "Security" (8-102)
q. "Security Certificate" (8-102)
r. "Security Entitlement" (8-102)
s. "Uncertificated Security" (8-102)

(4) Article 1 contains general definitions and principles of construction and interpretation applicable throughout this Article.

§9-106: "Accounts"; "General Intangibles":

1. **Accounts** -
   a) An Account is any right to payment:
      1) For goods sold or leased or for services rendered
      and 2) Which is not evidenced by an instrument or chattel paper, *whether or not it has been earned by performance*
   b) All rights to payment (earned or unearned) and incidental rights under a charter or other contract involving the use of hire of a vessel are considered to be accounts.

2. **General Intangibles** - Any personal property other than
   a) Goods
   b) Accounts
   c) Chattel Paper
   d) Documents
   e) Instruments
   f) Money
   g) Investment Property

§9-107: Purchase Money Security Interest ("PMSI") :

A PMSI is a S/I which has been:

(a) Taken or retained by the **seller** of collateral to secure all/part of its price

or (b) Taken by a person who advances money (or incurs an obligation) that enables the Debtor to buy the collateral (ex: financing bank) (Note: Money must be used to buy goods in order for the S/I to be effective as a PMSI)

§9-108: After-Acquired Property:

The S/I in the After-Acquired Property will be considered to have been taken for *New Value* (i.e. not as a Security for an Antecedent (prior) Debt) if:

a) The Secured Pty secures the After-Acquired Property by *either:*
- 1) Making an Advance
- or 2) Incurring an Obligation
- or 3) Releasing an already Perfected S/I
- or 4) Otherwise giving "New Value"

and b) The Debtor acquires rights in collateral *either:*
- 1) In the **Ordinary Course of Business**
- or 2) Under a **Contract of Purchase** made:
  - a. Pursuant to the S/A
  - and b. Within a reasonable time after *new value is given*

§9-109: Classification Of Goods:

(1) **Consumer Goods** - goods used or bought primarily for personal, family, or household purposes.

(2) **Equipment** - Goods are considered Equipment if

a) They are not included in the definitions of either
- 1) Inventory
- or 2) Consumer Goods
- or 3) Farming Products

and b) They are used or bought primarily for
- 1) Businesses (including farming or a profession)
- or 2) Non-Profit Organizations
- or 3) Governmental Agencies
- or 4) Farms

(3) **Farm Products** - Goods are considered Farming Products if
a) They are *either:*
1) Crops, livestock, or supplies used or produced in farming operations
or 2) Crops or livestock in their immature states (such as ginned cotton, wool-clip, maple syrup, milk, and eggs)
and b) They are in the possession of a Debtor who is engaged in either raising, fattening, grazing, or other farming operations.

*** Note: Goods which are Farm Products are neither Equipment nor Inventory.

(4) **Inventory** - Goods are considered Inventory if they are *either:*
a) Held by a person to be sold or leased
or b) To be furnished under service contracts
or c) Raw materials
or d) Work-In-Process or Materials used or consumed in business (i.e. inputs)

* *Principal Test: Are goods held for immediate or ultimate sale?*

§9-110: Sufficiency Of Description:

Description of Personal or Real Property need not be specific if it *reasonably identifies* what is described.

§9-111: Applicability Of Bulk Transfer Laws:

The creation of a Security Interest is not a Bulk Transfer under Article 6 (see §6-103).

§9-112: Where Collateral Is Not Owned By Debtor:

When a S/P knows that collateral is not owned by the Debtor, then, unless otherwise agreed, the Owner of the collateral:

1) Is entitled to receive any surplus from disposition (under §9-502(2) or §9-504(1))
2) Is not liable for any deficiency after resale
3) Has the same rights as the Debtor to:
    - (a) Receive Statements of Accounts or Lists of Collateral (as per §9-208)
    - and (b) Receive notice and object to a Secured Pty's proposal to retain collateral in satisfaction of the indebtedness (as per §9-505)
    - and (c) Redeem Collateral (as per §9-506)
    - and (d) Obtain injunctive or other relief (as per §9-507(1))
    - and (e) Recover losses caused by Secured Pty's failure to comply with a request to send Statements of Accounts or lists of Collateral (as per §9-208(2)).

§9-113: Security Interests Arising Under Article On Sales Or Article On Leases:

1) A S/I arising solely under Article 2 (Article on Sales) or Article 2A (Article on Leases) is subject to this Article as long as the Debtor does not have possession of the goods

2) Special Rules for S/I arising Article 2 or Article 2A:
    - (a) No Security Agreement is required to create an enforceable S/I.
    - and (b) Filing is not required to perfect the S/I.
    - and (c) Rights of Secured Pty upon Default - governed by
        - (i) Article 2 for S/I's arising solely under the Article of Sales
        - (ii) Article 2A for S/I's arising solely under the Article on Leases.

§9-114: Priority and Filing For Consignments: (see also §2-326):

(1) Priority of Consignors:

i) A person delivering goods under a Consignment which is not a S/I (and required to be filed as per §2-326(3)(c)) has priority over a Secured Pty of the Consignee who:

a) Has a perfected S/I in consignee's goods

and b) Has a S/I in identifiable Cash Proceeds (received on or before delivery of the goods to a buyer)

ii) This rule applies only if

(a) The Consignor **Files** (pursuant to §2-326(3)(c)) *before* the consignee receives possession of the goods.

and (b) Consignor gives **Written Notice** to all holders of a S/I if:

1. The S/I is in the *same type* of goods as those being consigned

2. The Secured Pty filed a F/S before Consignor files (or delivers goods)

and (c) The Secured Pty receives notification within 5 Yrs. before Consignee receives possession of consigned goods.

and (d) The Notification:

1. States that Consignor intends to deliver goods to Consignee on Consignment

and 2. Describes the goods (by item or type)

and e) The Consignment is not considered a S/I

and f) Filing is required (pursuant to §2-326(3)(c))

(2) A person delivering goods to another (i.e. consignor) becomes a *junior* Creditor to a Secured Pty who would have been perfected if:

a) The goods were property of the Debtor

and b) *Either:*

1. The Consignment is not a S/I

or 2. The above requirements have not been met

§2-326: Consignment:

(1) If delivered goods may be Returned by the "Buyer" (even though they conform), the transaction is considered *either:*

(a) A "**Sale on Approval**" - if the goods are delivered primarily for use (ex: trial period)

or (b) A "**Sale or Return**" - if the goods are delivered primarily for resale

(2) Effect of classification:(subject to (3) below)

a) "Sale on Approval" goods are not subject to "buyer's" creditors until goods are **accepted**

b) "Sale or Return" goods are subject to "buyer's" creditors while in the "buyer's" **possession**

(3) "Sale or Return"

i) Goods are deemed to be **"Sale or Return"** if:

a) Goods are delivered to a person for the purpose of resale

and b) The person (consignee) maintains a place of business (where he deals in goods of the kind involved)

and c) The Consignee sells the goods under a name other than the name of the person making the delivery (i.e. the Consignor).

ii) Form over Substance: These provisions apply even if:

a) Title is agreed not to pass until payment or resale

or b) The contract uses words such as "on consignment" or "on memorandum"

iii) <u>EXCEPTIONS to "Sale or Return" Classification</u>:

(a) The person making the delivery complies with an applicable law providing for consignor's interests to be *Evidenced by a Sign*.

or (b) The person making delivery establishes that the person conducting business is known by creditors to be *"substantially engaged in selling the goods of others"* (ex: a known auction house).

or (c) The person making delivery complies with filing provisions of Article 9.

(4) Any "or return" term of a contract for sale is considered

a) A separate contract for sale within the Statute of Frauds (§2-204)

and b) To be contradicting the sale aspect of the contract (within the provisions for parol or extrinsic evidence (as per §2-202))

§9-115: Investment Property:

(1) Definitions That Apply To This Article:

(a) **"Commodity account"** - An account maintained by a commodity intermediary in which a commodity contract is carried for a commodity customer.

(b) **"Commodity contract"** -

1. Types of Contracts Included:
   - a. A commodity futures contract
   - b. An option on a commodity futures contract
   - c. A commodity option
   - d. Other contract

2. Requirements - The Contract/Option must be:
   - (i) Traded on or subject to the rules of a board of trade that has been designated (pursuant to the federal commodities laws) as a contract market for such a contract
   - or (ii) Traded on a foreign commodity board of trade, exchange, or market, and is carried on the books of a commodity intermediary for a commodity customer.

(c) **"Commodity customer"** - A person for whom a commodity intermediary carries a commodity contract on its books.

(d) **"Commodity intermediary"** - includes:

(i) a person who is registered as a futures commission merchant under the federal commodities laws

or (ii) a person who in the *ordinary course of its business* provides clearance or settlement services for a board of trade that has been designated (pursuant to the federal commodities laws) as a contract market.

(e) "**Control**"

1. **Certificated Security, Uncertificated Security, Or Security Entitlement:** "Control" has the meaning specified in §8-106 with respect to:
   a. Certificated Securities
   b. Uncertificated Securities
   c. Security Entitlements

2. **Control Over Commodities Contract:**
   a. A secured party has control over a commodity contract if the commodity intermediary has agreed with the commodity customer and the secured party that it will apply any value distributed on account of the commodity contract as the secured party directs (without further consent by the commodity customer).
   b. If a commodity customer grants a security interest in a commodity contract to its own commodity intermediary, the commodity intermediary (who is the secured party) has control.

3. **Control Over Securities Account:** A secured party has control over a securities account or commodity account if the secured party has control over all security entitlements or commodity contracts carried in the securities account or commodity account.

(f) "**Investment property**" - includes:
(i) A security (whether certificated or uncertificated)
or (ii) A security entitlement
or (iii) A securities account
or (iv) A commodity contract
or (v) A commodity account

(2) **Effect of Attachment or Perfection of Security Interest:**

a. Attachment or Perfection of a security interest in a securities account is also considered Attachment or Perfection of a security interest in all security entitlements carried in the securities account.

b. Attachment or perfection of a security interest in a commodity account is also attachment or perfection of a security interest in all commodity contracts carried in the commodity account.

(3) **Description of Collateral:**

a. A description of collateral in a security agreement or financing statement is sufficient to create or perfect a security interest if it describes the collateral:

1. By its terms (see b. below)

or 2. As investment property

or 3. By description of the underlying security, financial asset, or commodity contract.

b. This applies to security interests created in:

1. A certificated security

or 2. An uncertificated security

or 3. A security entitlement

or 4. A securities account

or 5. A commodity contract

or 6. A commodity account

c. A description of investment property collateral in a security agreement or financing statement is sufficient if it identifies the collateral by:

1. Specific listing

or 2. Category

or 3. Quantity

or 4. A computational or allocational formula or procedure

or 5. Any other method, if the identity of the collateral is *objectively determinable*

(4) **Perfection:** Perfection of a security interest in investment property is governed by the following rules:

(a) **Perfection By Control:** A security interest in investment property may be perfected by control.

(b) **Perfection By Filing:** a security interest in investment property may be perfected by filing (except as otherwise provided in paragraphs (c) and (d)).

(c) **Perfection By Attachment:** If the debtor is a broker or securities intermediary, a security interest in investment property is perfected when it attaches (the filing of a financing statement with respect to a security interest in investment property granted by a broker or securities intermediary has no effect for purposes of perfection or priority with respect to that security interest).

(d) If a debtor is a commodity intermediary, a security interest in a commodity contract or a commodity account is perfected when it attaches (the filing of a financing statement with respect to a security interest in a commodity contract or a commodity account granted by a commodity intermediary has no effect for purposes of perfection or priority with respect to that security interest).

(5) **Priority:** To determine priority between conflicting security interests in the same investment property, use the following rules:

(a) **Control:** A security interest of a secured party who has control over investment property has priority over a security interest of a secured party who does not have control over the investment property.

(b) Conflicting security interests of secured parties who both have control rank equally (except as otherwise provided in paragraphs (c) and (d)).

(c) **Secured Party is Securities Intermediary:** A security interest in a security entitlement or a securities account granted to the debtor's own securities intermediary has priority over any security interest granted by the debtor to another secured party (except as otherwise agreed by the securities intermediary).

(d) **Secured Party is Commodity Intermediary:** A security interest in a commodity contract or a commodity account granted to the debtor's own commodity intermediary has priority over any security interest granted by the debtor to another secured party (except as otherwise agreed by the commodity intermediary).

(e) Conflicting security interests granted by a broker, a securities intermediary, or a commodity intermediary which are perfected without control rank equally.

(f) In all other cases, priority between conflicting security interests in investment property is governed by Section 9-312(5), (6), and (7). <u>§9-312(4) does not apply to investment property.</u>

(6) If a security certificate is delivered (in registered form) to a secured party pursuant to agreement, the following rules apply:

1. A written security agreement is <u>not required</u> for attachment or enforceability of the security interest.
2. Delivery suffices for perfection of the security interest.
3. The security interest has priority over a conflicting security interest perfected by means other than control, even if a necessary indorsement is lacking.

§9-116: Security Interest Arising in Purchase or Delivery of Financial Asset:

(1) **Purchase of Financial Assets:**

a. A securities intermediary has a security interest in the buyer's security entitlement securing the buyer's obligation to pay, if:

1. A person buys a financial asset through a securities intermediary.

and 2. The transaction is one in which the buyer is obligated to pay the purchase price to the securities intermediary *at the time of the purchase.*

and 3. The securities intermediary credits the financial asset to the buyer's securities account *before* the buyer pays the securities intermediary.

b. **Automatic Perfection:** A security agreement is <u>not required</u> for attachment or enforceability of the security interest, and the security interest is *automatically perfected.*

(2) **Delivery of Financial Assets:**

a. A person delivering a certificate (or other financial asset) has a security interest in the certificated security (or other financial asset) securing the seller's right to receive payment, if:

1. A certificated security (or other financial asset) is represented by a writing.

and 2. It is transferred by delivery with any necessary indorsement or assignment in the ordinary course of business.

and 3. It is delivered pursuant to an agreement between persons in the business of dealing with such securities or financial assets.

and 4. The agreement calls for delivery versus payment.

b. **Automatic Perfection:** A security agreement is <u>not required</u> for attachment or enforceability of the security interest, and the security interest is *automatically perfected.*

PART 2:

VALIDITY OF THE SECURITY AGREEMENT AND THE RIGHTS OF THE PARTIES

§9-201: General Validity Of Security Agreement:

1. A Security Agreement is effective according to its terms:
   a) Between the parties
   and b) Against purchasers of the collateral
   and c) Against creditors (i.e. other than a S/P)
   and d) Except as otherwise provided by the UCC

2. This Article Does Not:
   a) Validate illegal practices or charges (governed by statutes or regulations regarding usury, small loans, retail installment sales, or the like).
   b) Extend the application of any such statute or regulation to any transaction not otherwise subject to this Article.

§9-202: Title Of Collateral Immaterial:

Regardless of whether title to collateral is in the name of the Secured Pty or the Debtor, the provisions of this Article apply, with regard to a party's Rights, Obligations, and Remedies.

§9-203: Attachment And Enforceability Of Security Interest:

(1) **Requirements for Attachment**:

i) A Security Interest Attaches ONLY If:

(a) The collateral is **Secured** with *either:*
1. **Possession:** In the Possession of the Secured Pty (pursuant to agreement)

or 2. **Security Agreement:** Debtor has signed a Security Agreement which:
a. Is in WRITING
and b. Describes the Collateral (as per §9-110)
(Note: When collateral is crops or timber, a description of the land is required)

or 3. **Control of Investment Property** - If:
a. The collateral is INVENTMENT PROPERTY
and b. The Secured Pty has Control over the Investment Property (as per §9-115(1)(e))
and c. The Secured Pty is Controlling it pursuant to an agreement

and (b) **Value** has been given

and (c) **Debtor's Rights:** The Debtor has Rights in the collateral

ii) Requirements are subject to
a) §4-208 for Security Interests of a Collecting Bank
b) §9-115 and §9-116 for Security Interests in Investment Property
c) §9-113 for Security Interests arising under the Article of Sales (Article 2)

(2) **Time of Attachment**: A Security Interest attaches:

a) When it becomes enforceable against the Debtor (with respect to the collateral)

and b) *Either:*

i) As soon as the events specified in (1) take place **(they Must Coexist)**

or ii) When agreed (if agreement explicitly postpones the time of attachment)

(3) **Rights to Proceeds**: Secured Pty has the rights to Proceeds under §9-306 (i.e. no need to specify that proceeds will be covered by the S/A, unless otherwise agreed. You usually must specify if you do not want proceeds to be covered by the S/A).

(4) Transactions subject to this article are also subject to other statutes; those statutes shall supersede this article (ex: small loans, retail installment selling statutes, etc.).

§9-204: After-Acquired Property; Future Advances:

(1) A S/A may provide for After-Acquired Property to secure the obligations covered by the S/A (except as provided below in (2)).

(2) **Consumer Goods Exception:**

a) After-Acquired Property will not attach to a S/I if:

1. The S/I is in Consumer Goods

and 2. The After-Acquired Property is given as *additional* security

b) Exceptions: After-Acquired Property will attach in Consumer Goods if:

1. Debtor acquires rights in the After-Acquired Property within 10 Days after the Secured Pty gave value

or 2. They are Accessions (see §9-314)

(3) **Future Advances:**

a) Obligations covered by a S/A may include Future Advances or other value.

b) It is not necessary for the Future Advances to be given pursuant to a commitment (see 9-105(1)).

§9-205: Use Or Disposition Of Collateral Without An Accounting:

1) A S/I is NOT Invalid or Fraudulent, even if it:

a) Allows Debtor to:

1. Use, Commingle, or Dispose of all or part of the collateral

or 2. Collect or compromise Accounts or Chattel Paper

or 3. Accept returned goods

or 4. Make repossessions

or 5. Use, Commingle, or Dispose of Proceeds

or b) Does not require the Debtor to:

1. Account for proceeds

or 2. Replace collateral after disposition

2) This section does not relax the possession requirements for perfecting collateral.

§9-206: Agreement Not To Assert Defenses Against Assignee:

(1) Creating an Agreement Not to Assert Defenses Against Assignee:

a) An agreement by a Buyer (or Lessee) not to assert a Claim or Defense against an Assignee (which it may have against the Assignor of the Security Interest (seller/lessor)) is Enforceable if

1. The Assignee takes the assignment:

a. In Good Faith

and b. Paid Value for the assignment

and c. Without Notice of a Claim or Defense

and 2. The claim is not one which could be asserted against a Holder-In-Due Course (HDC) of a Negotiable Instrument (under Article 3)

b) A Buyer who signs *both* a Negotiable Instrument and a Security Agreement as part of *one* transaction makes an Agreement not to Assert Defenses Against an Assignee

c) This rule is subject to any statute/decision which establishes a different rule for buyers or lessees of consumer goods.

(2) Modification of Sales Warranties where Security Agreement Exists:
When a seller sells a PMSI in goods, Article 2 governs the sale and any disclaimer, limitation, or modification of the seller's warranties.

§9-207: Secured Party's Rights And Duties Over Collateral In Its Possession:

(1) **Secured Parties Obligation:**

a) **General Collateral:** A S/P must use *Reasonable Care* in the custody and preservation of the collateral in its possession.

b) **Instruments and Chattel Paper**: *Reasonable Care* includes taking the necessary steps to preserve rights against prior parties (unless otherwise agreed).

(2) **Rights and Duties of the S/P:** Unless parties otherwise agree, the following rights and duties apply when the S/P has Possession of the collateral:

(a) Reasonable Expectations: A Secured Pty may charge the Debtor (and be secured for) any *Reasonable Expenses* (including insurance, taxes, and other charges) incurred in the:

1. Custody of the collateral

or 2. Preservation of the collateral

or 3. Operation/use of the collateral

(b) Risk of Loss: If Insurance proceeds are insufficient, the Debtor shall bear the risk of Accidental Loss or Damage of the collateral.

(c) Value from the Collateral:

1. **Non-Monetary:** The S/P may hold any increase in value or profits (except money) received from the collateral as additional security for the debt.

2. **Money:** Money received from the collateral (as profits from its increased value) shall *either* be:

a) Returned to the Debtor

or b) Applied in reduction of the secured debt

(d) Identification of Collateral: If the collateral is not fungible, the S/P must keep it *identifiable* (fungible property may be commingled (ex: grain)).

(e) Re-pledging: The S/P may re-pledge the collateral if it does not impair the debtor's rights to redeem it.

(3) Although the S/P will be liable for any loss caused by his failure to comply with the above obligations, he will not lose his S/I.

(4) **Use of Collateral:** A S/P may use or operate the collateral if it is:
  a) For the purpose of preserving the collateral or its value
  or b) Pursuant to a court order (in the appropriate jurisdiction)
  or c) To the extent provided in the S/A (unless it's a Consumer Good)

§9-208: Request For A Statement Of Account Or List Of Collateral:

(1) **Confirming outstanding debt:**
  a) A Debtor may send a S/P a signed statement indicating the total amount he believes he owes (to a S/P as of a specified date), requesting that the S/P confirm or correct the stated balance.
  b) Debtor may also send the S/P a list of collateral to approve or correct (if the agreement (or other record) specifically identifies the collateral).

(2) **Answering The Request:**
  a) Secured Pty must send a written approval or correction within 2 weeks.
  b) If S/P claims a S/I in all of a particular type of collateral (ex: inventory), he only needs to indicate that he does (no need to approve each item separately).
  c) **Failure to comply:** If S/P fails to reply (without reasonable excuse):
    1) He is liable for any resulting loss caused to the Debtor.
    2) He is limited to the collateral listed in the Debtor's confirmation against persons *misled by his failure to comply* if the Debtor properly included:
      a. A *Good Faith Statement of his obligation*
      or b. A list of the collateral
  d) If the S/P no longer has the S/I (i.e. he assigned it):
    1) He must disclose the name and address of the new Secured Pty (if known to him)
    and 2) He is liable for any loss caused to the Debtor as a result of failing to disclose (as per §9-208)
  e) Successors of interest are not obligated to reply unless they personally received a request.

(3) The Debtor is entitled to such a statement once every 6 Months, without charge (each additional statement may not exceed a $10.00 charge).

PART 3:

PRIORITIES AND RIGHTS OF PARTIES:

§9-301: Priority Over Unperfected Security Interests:

(1) Classes of People who take Priority over an Unperfected Security Interest:

(a) A **Perfected S/P** entitled to priority under §9-312

or (b) A person who becomes a **Lien Creditor** *before* the Security Interest is Perfected (but see (2))

or (c) **A Buyer:** Requirements to qualify as a "Buyer":

1) The Buyer must be *either:*

a) A Buyer not in the Ordinary Course of Business

or b) A Bulk Transferee

or c) A Buyer of Farm Products - in the Ordinary Course of Business

and 2) The Buyer cannot be a Secured Pty.

and 3) The Buyer must:

a) Have *No Knowledge* of the S/I

and b) Give *Value*

and c) *Receive delivery* (of collateral) before the S/I is perfected

and 4) The Collateral must either be:

a) Goods

or b) Instruments

or c) Documents

or d) Chattel Paper

or (d) **Transferee of Accounts, General Intangibles or Investment Property** who:

1) Gives value before they are perfected

and 2) Is without knowledge of S/I

and 3) Is not a Secured Pty

(2) **PMSI Exception:** A Secured Pty takes priority over any Lien Creditor or "Bulk Transferee" (whose rights arise between the time of attachment and filing) if the Secured Pty files a PMSI:

a) Before Debtor receives the collateral (i.e. before attachment)

or b) Within 10 Days after Debtor receives **Possession** of the collateral

(3) A **Lien Creditor** is

a) A Creditor who obtains a Lien on property involved *by attachment, levy,* or the like

or b) An Assignee for the Benefit of Creditors from the time of assignment

or c) A Trustee in Bankruptcy from the date of the filing of the petition

or d) A Receiver in Equity from the time of appointment

(4) A person who becomes a Lien Creditor after a S/I is perfected, takes subject to that S/I only if it:

a) Secures **Future Advances** made to Debtor:

1. Before the Third Pty becomes a Lien Creditor

or 2. Within 45 Days *after* the Third Pty becomes a Lien Creditor

or b) Is made **Without Knowledge** of the Lien

or c) Is made pursuant to a **Prior Commitment** entered into *without knowledge* of the lien

§9-302: When Filing Is Not Required:

(1) A **Financing Statement** **MUST BE FILED** to perfect all S/I's, **UNLESS** it is:

(a) A S/I in Collateral which is already **in Possession** of the Secured Pty (pursuant to §9-305)

or (b) A S/I **Temporarily Perfected,** *either:*

1. In instruments, documents, or Certificated Securities without delivery (as per §9-304 - 21 Day rule)

or 2. In proceeds for a 10 Day period (as per §9-306)

or (c) A S/I created by an Assignment of a Beneficial Interest in a Trust (or a decedents estate)

or (d) **A PMSI in <u>CONSUMER GOODS</u>,** unless it is for
1. Motor Vehicles required to be registered
or 2. Fixtures (as per §9-313)

or (e) An **<u>Assignment of Accounts</u>,** which does not transfer a significant part of the assignor's accounts (alone or in conjunction with other assignments to the same Assignee)

or (f) A S/I
1. Of a Collecting Bank (§4-208)
or 2. Arising under Article 2 (Article on Sales) (as per §9-113)
or 3. Covered in (3) below

or (g) **An Assignment:**
1. For the benefit of all creditors of the transferor
and 2. Subsequent transfers by the Assignee

or (h) **An Investment Property:**
1. The Security Interest is in <u>Investment Property</u>
and 2. It is perfected without filing (as per §9-115 or §9-116)

(2) If a Perfected S/I is assigned, re-filing is not required to continue perfection against the original debtor's creditors.

(3) Filing is NOT Required to perfect a S/I in property already subject to:

(a) **A U.S. Statute/Treaty** providing for

1. International/national Registration

or 2. An international/national Certificate of Title

or 3. A specific place of filing (different than UCC)

or (b) **A Certificate of Title Statute** or **Central Filing Statute,** *unless* the collateral is **Inventory** held by a *"Merchant"* (a person in the business of selling those kinds of goods) - in which UCC filing (as per Part 4) applies

or (c) A Certificate of Title statute (of another jurisdiction) requiring that the S/I be stated on the certificate to be perfected (ex: automobiles).

(4) When complying with any statute/treaty in (3), a S/I will be subject to the UCC in *all but the following areas:*

a) Filing pursuant to a statute - will be equivalent to filing a financing statement under Article 9

b) Perfection - will be subject to those particular statutes, except as provided in §9-103 for Multi-State transactions

c) Duration/Renewal of perfection - will be governed by the statute

§9-303: Perfection:

(1) A S/I is Perfected when it has Attached to the collateral AND either

a) All of the required steps for perfection have been taken as specified in *either:*

1. §9-302 (Perfection by Filing)

or 2. §9-304 (Perfection of Instruments)

or 3. §9-305 (Perfection by Possession)

or 4. §9-306 (Perfection in Proceeds)

or 5. §9-115 (Perfection of Investment Property)

or b) If the required steps (above) are taken before attachment, the Security Interest attaches

(2) **Continuous Perfection**: The S/I shall be deemed to be Perfected Continuously (for purposes of Article 9) if:

a) A S/I is originally perfected in any way (permitted under Article 9)

and b) The S/I is *subsequently* perfected (renewed) in some other way (under Article 9)

and c) There was no intermediate time when the S/I was not perfected

§9-304: Perfection Of Instruments:

(1) Perfecting Instruments

a) A S/I in Chattel Paper or Negotiable Documents may be perfected by filing.

b) A S/I in Money or Instruments (other than chattel paper) can only be perfected by **Possession** *unless:*

1) It is an Instrument which is **temporarily perfected** under §9-304(4) or (5)

2) It is Proceeds, which is **temporarily perfected** under §9-306(2) or (3)

(2) Perfecting Documents of Goods

- a) When goods are in the possession of an issuer of a Negotiable Document (representing the goods), the Goods may be perfected by perfecting a S/I in the document.
- b) Any other S/I in the goods (i.e. perfected in any other way) will be subject to the S/I in the document

(3) Perfecting Permissive Filings

- a) If Goods are in the possession of a *Bailee* (other than the issuer of a Negotiable Document), they may be perfected by *either:*
  - 1) The issuance of a Document in the name of the Secured Pty
  - or 2) A Receipt by the Bailee with a *notification* of the Secured Pty's interest
  - or 3) By filing as to the goods
- b) If a Bailee has issued a Negotiable Document for the goods, §9-304(2) applies.

(4) Temporary Perfection Without Filing

- a) A S/I is automatically perfected for 21 Days from the time of **attachment** (even without proper filing or possession) for:
  - 1) Instruments
  - and 2) Negotiable Documents (only includes goods in a Bailee's possession if it made a Negotiable Document for those goods)
  - and 3) Certificated Securities
- b) Requirements for Automatic Temporary perfection:
  - 1) The S/I must arise under a *written* Security Agreement
  - and 2) *New value* must be given for the S/I

(5) Continued Perfection when Collateral is Given to Debtor

A S/I remains perfected for 21 Days (without filing) if

1) A Secured Pty has a Perfected S/I in:

a) An Instrument

or b) A Negotiable Document

or c) Goods in the possession of a Bailee

or d) Certificated Security

and 2) The S/P has:

(a) Made available Goods or Documents to the Debtor for the purpose of:

1) Ultimate Sale or Exchange

or 2) Loading/Unloading/Storing

or 3) Shipping/Transshipping

or 4) Manufacturing/Processing

or 5) Dealing with them in a manner preliminary to sale/exchange

**** Note: Priority between conflicting S/I's in goods are subject to §9-312(3)

or (b) Delivered Instruments or Certificated Securities to the Debtor for the purpose of:

1) Ultimate sale or exchange

or 2) Presentation (for sale)

or 3) Collection

or 4) Renewal

or 5) Registration of Transfer

(6) After the 21 Day Period, the S/I must be perfected by complying with the applicable provisions in Article 9 if:

a) It is still not perfected (as per (4))

or b) It is still in debtor's possession (as per (5))

§9-305: Perfecting By Possession:

1) Possession may be used to perfect a S/I in:
   a) Letters of Credit (as per §5-116)
   or b) Goods
   or c) Instruments
   or d) Money
   or e) Negotiable Documents
   or f) Chattel Paper

2) **Time of Possession with Bailee**: If Collateral is held by a Bailee, the Secured Pty is deemed to have possession when the Bailee *receives notification* of the Secured Pty's interest (unless the Bailee issues a Negotiable Document for the goods).

3) Perfection begins at the time of Possession (No Relation Back), and *continues* only as long as possession is retained (unless otherwise specified in UCC (ex: §9-304(5)'s 21 Day rule)).

4) The S/I can otherwise be Perfected Before or After possession only as provided by other sections of the UCC.

§9-306: Rights In "Proceeds":

(1) **"Proceeds"**

a) Proceeds may be obtained from:

1. Whatever is received upon:
   a. Sale
   or b. Exchange
   or c. Collection
   or d. Other disposition (of collateral or proceeds)

or 2. Insurance payable from the loss/damage of the collateral, *unless* the insurance check is made payable to a non-party of the security agreement (Note: can be endorsed by Third Pty to become valid)

or 3. Any payments or distributions made with respect to investment property collateral.

b) Proceeds may be in the form of:

1. **Cash Proceeds** - Money, checks, deposit accounts, etc.

or 2. **Non-Cash Proceeds** - all other proceeds

(2) **Continuation of the S/I:** Unless otherwise provided by the UCC, a S/I in collateral continues in:

a) Collateral - even if it is sold/disposed of, unless the disposition was *authorized* by the Secured Pty

and b) Proceeds - ONLY if the proceeds are IDENTIFIABLE

(3) **The Security Interest in Proceeds**

i) A S/I in Proceeds is considered *Continuously Perfected* if the original collateral was "re-perfected" within 10 Days (of "conversion" to proceeds) (i.e. the date of perfection in the Proceeds relates back to date the original collateral was perfected).

ii) The Proceeds becomes unperfected 10 Days after the Debtor receives the proceeds - Unless they are "re-perfected" (within the 10 day period).

iii) A S/I in proceeds can only be perfected by the rules spelled out in the UCC, for *original collateral of the same type*.

iv) Perfection can be continuously maintained in Proceeds if:

(a) **AUTOMATIC RE-PERFECTION** occurs; Automatic re-perfection occurs if *either:*

1. Non-Cash Proceeds: (ex: a car for a car)

a. The *filed* Financing Statement covers the original collateral

and b. The proceeds are collateral in which a S/I may be perfected by filing (i.e. not cash) in the office where the Financing Statement was filed (even if you don't re-file) (Default Rule: silence means you have a S/I in proceeds)

or 2. Non-Cash Proceeds bought with Cash Proceeds: If the *non-cash proceeds on* are acquired with ***cash- proceeds***, perfection continues if the Financing Statement indicates the types of property constituting the proceeds (ex: a car for cash, to buy a new car).

or (b) Proceeds are **CASH PROCEEDS** (ex: Accounts), AND:

1. Cash-proceeds are identifiable

and 2. A *filed* Financing Statement covers the original collateral

or (c) The original collateral was Investment Property and the proceeds are Identifiable Cash proceeds

or (d) The S/I in the proceeds is perfected before the *10 Day* period expires.

(4) S/I In Proceeds of an Insolvent Debtor - A S/P (with a perfected S/I in proceeds) can only maintain a S/I in:

(a) **Non-Cash Proceeds**, which are
1. Identifiable
and 2. In a separate deposit account, containing only proceeds

or (b) **Money Cash-Proceeds**, which are
1. Identifiable
and 2. In the form of money
and 3. Not commingled with other money
and 4. Not deposited into a deposit account *prior* to insolvency

or (c) **Instrument Cash-Proceeds** (i.e. checks, notes), which are
1. Identifiable
and 2. Not deposited in a deposit account *prior* to insolvency proceedings

or (d) **Cash-Proceeds in Accounts** - In all cash and deposit accounts of the Debtor (in which proceeds have been commingled) perfection may be maintained, yet it will be:
(i) Subject to any right to set-off
and (ii) Limited to:

An "Amount" (<= any cash-proceeds received by Debtor within 10 days of insolvency) less - (I) Payments to S/P on "account of cash proceeds" (within 10 Day period) less - (II) Cash Proceeds received by Debtor during 10 Day period

(5) Priorities with Returned/Repossessed Goods

i) **Requirements for Priority:**

a) The Sale of goods must result in an Account or Chattel Paper which is transferred by the seller to the S/P.

and b) The goods must be *returned* or *repossessed* by the Debtor or the S/P.

ii) **Rules of Priorities for Returned/Repossessed Goods**

(a) RE-PERFECTION: The Original Security Interest *re-attaches* to the goods, continuing perfection if:

1. The goods were collateral at the time of the sale

and 2. The debt attached to collateral not paid at the sale

and 3. It was perfected when the goods were sold

and 4. *Either:*

a. If **Perfection by Filing:** S/P files a new F/S *only* if the original Filing is not still effective

or b. If **Non-Filed Perfection:** S/P takes possession of goods or file a new F/S

(b) CHATTEL PAPER:

1. An unpaid Transferee of the Chattel Paper maintains a S/I in the goods against the transferor.

2. If Transferee of Chattel Paper is entitled to priority (pursuant to §9-308), then he takes priority over RE-PERFECTED Secured Ptys (see (a)above).

(c) ACCOUNTS:

1. An unpaid Transferee of an account has a S/I in goods against the Transferor.

2. This S/I is *subordinate* to a re-perfected S/I (see (a) above)

(d) A S/I of an unpaid transferee (pursuant to (b) and (c)) must be perfected to protect themselves against

1. Creditors of the Transferor

and 2. Purchasers of the returned/repossessed goods

§9-307: Protection Of Buyers Of Goods:

(1) A BUYER IN THE ORDINARY COURSE OF BUSINESS
- a) A "BIOC" takes FREE of any S/I even if
    - 1) The S/I is perfected
    - and 2) The buyer knows of its existence
- b) **Requirement:** The S/I must have been created by the seller (i.e. the seller must be the original Debtor)
- c) Exception: This section does not apply to people buying farm products from a person engaged in farming operations.

(2) CONSUMER GOODS (Consumer to Consumer): Buyer takes free and clear if
- a) He buys without knowledge of S/I
- and b) He buys for Value
- and c) He buys it for his own personal, family, or household use
- and d) The S/P did not file a financing statement *before* consumer purchased

(3) OTHER BUYERS: (Not Ordinary Course of Business):
- a) A Buyer takes free of Future Advances covered by a S/I only if the Future Advances are made *before* the *earlier* of:
    - 1. The time that the S/P acquires knowledge of the purchases
    - or 2. 45 Days after the purchase
- b) A Buyer will NOT take free of Future Advances if they are made Pursuant to a Commitment entered into:
    - 1. Without knowledge of the purchase
    - and 2. Before the expiration of the 45 day period

§9-308: Chattel Paper and Instruments:

Purchasers of Chattel Paper or Instruments take Priority over a S/I in that Chattel Paper or Instrument if the purchaser takes it:

(a) **Without Knowledge of S/I**: To maintain priority, the Purchaser must prove that:

1. Purchaser took *without knowledge* that the Chattel Paper or Instrument is subject to a S/I

and 2. New Value was given for it

and 3. He took Possession of the Chattel Paper in the Ordinary Course of his Business

and 4. It is Perfected under *either:*

a) §9-304 (permissive filing and temporary perfection)

or b) §9-306 (perfection as to proceeds)

or (b) **With Knowledge**: To maintain priority, the Purchaser must prove that:

1. The Instrument or Chattel Paper is *Proceeds of Inventory*, subject to a S/I (as per §9-306) even though he knows that the specific Chattel Paper or Instrument. is subject to a S/I

and 2. New Value was given for it

and 3. He took Possession of the Chattel Paper in the *Ordinary Course of his Business*

§9-309: Protection Of Purchasers Of Instruments, Documents, And Securities:

1. Article 9 does NOT limit the rights of a:

a) Holder In Due Course of a Negotiable Instrument (§3-302)

or b) Holder to whom a Negotiable Document has been duly Negotiated (§7-501)

or c) A *Protected Purchaser* of a security (§8-303)

2. Such Holders or Purchasers Take Priority over an *earlier* (and, of course, later), S/I (even if perfected).

3. Filing under Article 9 does NOT constitute Notice to such holders/Purchasers.

§9-310: Priority Of Certain Liens Arising By Operation Of Law:

1) A person will have a Lien on goods if:
    a) She furnishes services or materials for the secured goods
    and b) It is done in the Ordinary Course of his business
    and c) she retains Possession of the goods
    and d) There is a Statute or Rule of law creating a lien for such services or materials

2) This Possessory, Statutory Lien will take Priority over a Perfected S/I *unless:*
    a) The lien arises only by Statute
    and b) The Statute expressly provides otherwise

§9-311: Alienability Of Debtor's Rights:

1) The Debtor's rights in the collateral may be *voluntarily* or *involuntarily* transferred by:
    a) Sale
    or b) Creation of another Security Interest
    or c) Attachment
    or d) Levy
    or e) Garnishment
    or f) Other Judicial Process

2) The Debtor may transfer his rights even if the S/A prohibits such a transfer or makes the transfer constitute a default.

§9-312: Priorities Among Conflicting Security Interests In The Same Collateral:

(Between Perfected S/P's only; for other priority conflicts see §9-301)

(1) **Scope:** Rules stated in other sections of Part 3, as well as the following other sections of the UCC shall govern when applicable:

- a) §4-208 (S/I of Collecting Banks in items being collected, accompanying documents, and proceeds)
- b) §9-103 (S/I related to other jurisdictions)
- c) §9-114 (Consignments)
- d) §9-115 (S/I in Investment Property)

(2) **S/I in Crops**:

a) A Perfected S/I in crops takes priority over an earlier perfected S/I if:

1. The New Creditor gave value to enable Debtor to produce the crops during the production season

and 2. The New Creditor gave money within 3 Mos. before the crops become "growing crops" (ex: by planting them)

and 3. The Earlier S/I secures obligations due more than 6 Months before crops became "growing crops"

b) It is irrelevant that New Creditor had knowledge of earlier S/I.

(3) **PMSI Super-Priority in INVENTORY:**

i) A Perfected PMSI in inventory has Priority over a conflicting S/I in the same inventory.

ii) PMSI "Super-Priority" applies Only to:

a) The same inventory

and b) Identifiable **cash proceeds** received on or before the day that Debtor delivers the inventory to a Third Pty buyer (OK if proceeds are money, checks, deposit accounts; No good if converted to cash proceeds; must be direct cash proceeds (ex: car-trade-ins are not good, Accounts receivable and Chattel Paper are also no good))

iii) Requirements for PMSI Priority

(a) The PMSI is perfected when Debtor receives possession of inventory.

and (b) The "Purchase Money" Secured Pty *gives written notice* to the conflicting Secured Pty only if the conflicting Secured Pty filed a financing statement covering the same types of inventory *before:*

(i) The "Purchase Money" Secured Pty filed (or Debtor receives Possession)

or (ii) The beginning of the 21 Day period (in which a PMSI is temporarily perfected without filing or possession (as per §9-304(5)))

and (c) The Conflicting Secured Pty received the notification within 5 Yrs before the Debtor receives possession of the inventory (i.e. since a notice is effective for 5 Yrs, S/P can continue making PMSI's without further notices within 5 yr. period)

and (d) The notice states that the person sending it expects to obtain a PMSI in the debtor's Inventory (describing the inventory by or type)

(4) **A PMSI in Non-Inventory Collateral** (ex: Equipment):

A Purchase-Money-Secured Pty has priority over conflicting secured parties in collateral or its proceeds if the:

a. PMSI is perfected at the time Debtor receives possession of the collateral

or b. PMSI is perfected within 10 Days after Debtor receives possession of collateral

(5) **First in Time, First in Right**: In all other cases (not specified above), priority between conflicting S/I's in the same collateral shall be determined according to the following rules:

(a) **First to Perfect:**

1. Conflicting S/I's Rank according to priority in Time of Filing or Perfection.
2. Priority dates back from the *earlier* of the first Perfection **or** Filing as long as later there is no period in which there is neither filing nor perfection (i.e. it is continuous).

(b) **The First to Attach** the collateral, if all conflicting S/I's are unperfected.

(6) The date of Filing/Perfection for collateral is the same date to apply to Proceeds of that collateral (for purposes for §9-312(5)).

(7) **Future Advances:**

a) A S/P will maintain the SAME PRIORITY (under (5) above or §9-115(5)) in *Future Advances* (as per §9-301(4)) as he did in his *original advance* (loan) if the Future Advances are made:

1) **After** the original S/I is perfected (by filing or possession (or under §9-115 or §9-116 on Investment property))

or 2) **Before/while** the S/I is perfected

b) In all other cases, a perfected S/I has priority from the date the advance was made (i.e. if you perfect collateral worth $10M and initial lien is for $2M (covering a $2M cash advancement), a subsequent advance for $6M will have the same priority as the first loan's lien).

§9-313: Priority In Fixtures:

(1) **General Definitions**

(a) Goods are "**Fixtures**" when they become so related to *particular* Real Estate that an interest in them arises under Real Estate Law.

(b) A "**Fixture Filing**" is a filing of a financing statement for fixture goods in the office where Real Estate mortgages are filed or recorded (pursuant to §9-402(5)).

(c) A "**Constructive Mortgage**" is a mortgage that secures an obligation incurred for the *construction of an improvement* on the land (If the recorded writing indicates, the Constructive mortgage may include the cost to acquire the land).

(2) **Security Interests in Fixtures:**

a) A Security Interest in Fixtures:

1. May be created in goods which are fixtures

and 2. May *continue* in goods which become fixtures

b) A S/I may not be created (under Article 9) in ordinary building materials incorporated into an improvement on land.

(3) This Article does not prevent the creation of a fixture lien ("encumbrance") pursuant to the state's Real Estate law

(4) **Priority of a Perfected Fixture S/I:** A Perfected S/I in fixtures has *priority* over a conflicting interest of the Owner or a lien-holder of the Real Property ("Encumbrancer") only if the Fixture S/I is:

(a) **A PMSI** only if:

1. The goods become fixtures *after* the Owner's or the Encumbrancer's interest arises

and 2. The S/I is perfected by **Fixture Filing**

a) Before the goods became fixtures

or b) Within 10 Days after they became fixtures

and 3. The Debtor has

a) Possession of the Real Estate

or b) A Recorded interest in the Real Estate

or (b) **Filed First** only if:
1. The S/I was perfected by Fixture Filing *before* the Owner or Encumbrancer recorded their interests

and 2. The S/I has priority over any conflicting interest of a predecessor in the Owner or Encumbrancer's title

and 3. The Debtor has
a) Possession of the Real Estate
or b) A Recorded interest in the Real Estate

or (c) **In Removable Fixtures** only if:
1. The fixtures are:
a) Readily removable factory or office machines
or b) Readily removable replacements of Domestic Appliances (which are consumer goods)

and 2. The S/I was perfected *before* the goods became fixtures (by any method allowed by this Article)

or (d) **A Judicial Lien** only if the conflicting interest is a judicial lien on the Real Estate, obtained *after* the S/I was perfected (by any method allowed by this Article (ex: judgment obtained in a court of law))

(5) **Priority of an Unperfected Fixture S/I:** A S/I in fixtures, *whether or not perfected*, has Priority over a conflicting Owner or Encumbrancer of Real Estate if:

(a) The Owner or Encumbrancer has
1. Consented in writing to the S/I
or 2. Disclaimed an interest in the goods as fixtures

or (b) The Debtor has a right to remove the goods as against the Owner or Encumbrancer.
(Note: If the Debtor loses this right, the priority of the S/I continues for a "reasonable time").

(6) **Priority Against Construction Mortgages:**

a) A S/I in fixtures is Subordinate to a **Construction Mortgage** if:

1. The Construction Mortgage was recorded *before* the goods became Fixtures

and 2. The goods became fixtures *before* the completion of the construction

b) If a Mortgage is given to refinance a Construction Mortgage it has the same priority as the Construction Mortgage.

c) This section is subject to (4) and (5) above, but not subsection (4)(a) for PMSI Fixtures.

(7) **All Other Cases:**

a) In all other cases not within the preceding subsections, a S/I in Fixtures is Subordinate to the Owner's or Encumbrancer's conflicting interest in the fixtures.

b) This rule (9-313(7)) only applies if the Owner or Encumbrancer is NOT the Debtor.

(8) **Removal of Collateral Upon Default**

a) If a S/P has priority over all Owners and Encumbrancers, he may remove his collateral from the Real Estate if the Debtor defaults (subject to Part 5).

b) **Reimbursement:**

1. The S/P Must *reimburse* any Encumbrancer or Owner of the Real Estate for the cost to repair any *physical injury* resulting from the removal if:

   a The Owner or Encumbrancer is not the Debtor

   or b. The Owner or Encumbrancer has not otherwise greed

2. The S/P need NOT Reimburse the Owner or Encumbrancer for:

   a. Any loss in value of the Real Estate cause by the absence of the removed goods

   or b. The loss incurred by any necessity of *replacing* the goods

3. Those parties entitled to reimbursement may *refuse* permission for the S/P to remove his collateral until he gives them *adequate security* that he will reimburse them for the appropriate damages.

§9-314: Accessions:

(1) **Security Interest Attached Before Installation**

a. A S/P with an interest in goods ("input goods") which attach *before* they become installed or affixed to other goods retains priority over those input goods, against claims over the "whole" (i.e. the goods which they are attached to).

b. In order to maintain priority, the S/I must *attach* to the goods before they are installed or affixed to other goods (i.e. the "whole").

c. The S/I in the original, input goods takes *priority* over any party's claim in the Whole (i.e. the final product), subject to:

a) §9-315(1) (Commingled Goods)

b) §9-314(3) (Exceptions)

(2) **Security Interest Attached After Installation**

a. A S/I attached to Accessions (i.e. the original, input goods) *after* they become part of a Whole is **valid** against any subsequent S/I's in the Whole (subject to the exceptions in (3) below).

b. The S/I is **invalid** against anyone with a S/I in the Whole *before* the S/I attaches to the Accessions, *unless* the S/P with an interest in the Whole *either:*

1. **Consents** *in writing* to the S/I in the Accessions

or 2. **Disclaims** *in writing* its interest in the Accessions as part of the whole.

(3) **Exceptions**: The S/I's described above in (1) and (2) do not take priority over:

(a) A "*Subsequent Purchaser,*" if he buys:

1. Any interest in the Whole for **value**

and 2. **Without Knowledge** of the S/I

and 3. ***Before*** the S/I in the Accessions is perfected

(**** Note: A Purchaser of the Whole at a foreclosure sale is considered to be a "Subsequent Purchaser" within this section (unless the purchaser is the holder of a perfected S/I , buying at his own foreclosure sale))

(b) A Judicial Lien Creditor, if:

1. A Lien on the Whole is *subsequently* obtained by judicial proceedings

and 2. The Lien is obtained **Without Knowledge** of the S/I

and 3. The Lien is obtained *before* the S/I in the Accessions is perfected

(c) Future Advances if:

1. Creditor making Future Advances has a Prior Perfected S/I in the Whole

and 2. Creditor *contracts for* or *makes* Future Advances **Without Knowledge** of the S/I

and 3. Creditor *contracts for* or *makes* Future Advance *before* the S/I in the input goods is Perfected.

(4) **Removal of Collateral Upon Default**

a. If a S/P's interest in the accessions has priority over *all* other Secured Parties with interests in the Whole (pursuant to (1), (2), and (3) above), he may remove his collateral from the Whole if the Debtor defaults (subject to Part 5).

b. The S/P must reimburse any Encumbrancer or Owner of the Whole for the cost to repair any *physical injury* resulting from the removal of the collateral if:

1 The Owner or Encumbrancer is not the Debtor

or 2. The Owner or Encumbrancer has not otherwise agreed

c. The S/P need NOT Reimburse the Owner or Encumbrancer for

1. Any loss in value of the Whole caused by the absence of the removed goods

or 2. The loss incurred by any necessity of *replacing* the goods

d. Those entitled to reimbursement may *refuse* permission for the S/P to remove his collateral until he gives them *adequate security* that he will reimburse them for the appropriate damages.

§9-315: Priority When Goods Which Are Commingled Or Processed:

(1) If a S/I in goods is perfected, and those goods are *later* used as inputs for end products, the S/I continues in those end products if:

(a) The identity of the goods are lost - in the end product

or (b) A Financing Statement covering the *Original Goods* also covers the end product (which the input goods have been placed into)

(Note: A separate S/I in the inputs (as per §9-314) may not be taken in addition to the S/I in the end products (i.e. choice of one or the other))

(2) If there are different S/I's in the different goods which form the end product (ex: X has a $100 perfected S/I in cotton and Y has a $200 perfected S/I in the polyester. The debtor converts this into $600 worth of shirts. X has an interest of 1/6 and Y has an interests of 2/6), then the S/I's rank **Equally** according to the Ratio of:

$$\frac{\textbf{Cost of Original Goods}}{\textbf{Cost of End Product}}$$

§9-316: Priority Agreements:

Parties may agree to subordinate their priorities to other parties.

§9-317: Secured Party Not Obligated On Contract Of Debtor:

A S/P does not incur Contract and Tort liability for the *Debtor's* acts or omissions, simply because of:

1) The mere existence of a S/I

or 2) The Authority given to the Debtor to dispose of or use the Collateral

§9-318: Assignments:

(1) Defenses Against Assignees: Unless the Account Debtor has made an enforceable agreement not to assert Defenses or Claims arising out of a sale (as per §9-206), the rights of an Assignee are subject to:

(a) **Contractual Terms:** All Terms of the Contract between the Account Debtor and Assignor, *including* any Claim or Defense arising from the contract

(b) **"Set Offs"** (outside contact): Any other defense or claim that the Account Debtor has against the Assignor, as long as it accrues *before* the Account Debtor received notification of the assignment.

(2) Modification of Contract After Notification of Assignment

a. Any Modification of or Substitution for the Contract will be effective against the Assignee, *whether or not notification of assignment has been given,* if:

1. It is made in Good Faith

and 2. It is in accordance with *Reasonable Commercial Standards*

and 3. The Right to Payment has not been fully earned by performance under the assigned contract

and 4. The Account Debtor has not otherwise agreed

b. The Assignee acquires the Assignor's corresponding rights under the Modified or Substituted Contract.

c. The Assignment may provide that such a Modification or Substitution is a breach by the Assignor if a Perfected S/I is assigned.

(3) Identification and Proof of Assignment

a. The Account Debtor is Authorized to pay the *Assignor* until the Account Debtor receives notice that:

1. An assignment has been made

and 2. That payment shall be made to the Assignee

b. A Notification which does not *reasonably identify* the rights assigned to the Assignee is *ineffective*

c. The Account Debtor may continue to pay the Assignor until the Assignee provides *reasonable proof* (upon Debtor's request) that the assignment has actually been made.

(4) Term Prohibiting Assignment Ineffective: A Term in any contract between an Account Debtor and an Assignor is *ineffective* if it:

a. Prohibits the Assignment of an account

or b. Prohibits the creation of a S/I in a general intangible for money due or to become due

or c. Requires the Account Debtor's consent for such assignment or S/I

PART 4:

FILING

§9-401: Place Of Filing (INTRASTATE):

(1) **Place of Filing:** The proper place, within a state, to file in order to perfect a S/I:

ALTERNATIVE I

(a) Office where Real Estate Mortgage would be filed for:

1. Natural Resources (oil, gas, minerals, timber)
2. Accounts subject to §9-103(5)
3. Fixture Financing Statement (as per §9-313) for goods which are (or will become) fixtures

(b) Office of the Secretary of State - for all other goods

ALTERNATIVE II

(a) In the County where Debtor lives (or where goods are kept if Debtor is not a resident of the state) for:

1) Farming Equipment or Products
2) General Intangibles arising/relating to the sale of farm products/equipment
3) Consumer goods
4) Growing Crops, or crops to be grown (must also file in county where land is located)

(b) Office where Real Estate Mortgage would be filed for:

1. Natural Resources (oil, gas, minerals, timber)
2. Accounts subject to §9-103(5)
3. Fixture Financing Statement (as per §9-313) for goods which are (or will become) fixtures

(c) Office of the Secretary of State - for all other goods

ALTERNATIVE III

(a) In the County where Debtor lives (or where goods are kept if Debtor is not a resident of the state) for:

1) Farming Equipment or Products
2) General Intangibles arising/relating to the sale of Farm Products/Equipment
3) Consumer Goods
4) Growing Crops - or crops to be grown (must also file in county where land is located)

(b) Office where Real Estate Mortgage would be filed for:

1) Natural Resources (oil, gas, minerals, timber)
2) Accounts subject to §9-103(5)
3) Fixture Financing Statement (as per §9-313) for goods which are (or will become) fixtures

(c) Office of the Secretary of State - for **all other goods,** *plus,* must also file:

1) In the county where the Debtor does business (if Debtor only does business in one county in the state)

or 2) In the County where Debtor resides (if Debtor resides in state but has no place of business in state)

(2) **Erroneous Filing** (within the correct State):

a) Erroneous Filings are still *effective* (but not perfected) with regard to:

1) Any of the collateral as to which the filing did comply with the filing requirements (of the UCC) (ex- if some of the collateral under the Security Agreement was properly filed, that collateral is protected (i.e. the entire Security Agreement is not ineffective))

and 2) Collateral covered by the Financing Statement against anyone who knew the contents of it

b) In order for an Erroneous Filing to be effective:

1) It must have been made in Good Faith and *either:*

a) Is filed in an improper place in the proper state

or b) Is not filed in all the required places

or 2) Future Secured Ptys have **Actual Knowledge** of erroneous filing (Note: Lien-holders and trustees in bankruptcy usually don't have knowledge, since they are not required to look at file)

(3) **Removal of Collateral**

Creditor need not re-file (to continue the effectiveness of the original filing) even if:

1. The use of the collateral changes

or 2. The collateral is moved (or either debtor's residence or place of business changes (whichever determined where to originally file)) .

ALTERNATIVE

a) Filing made in the proper county continues to be effective for up to 4 Months. after Debtor/collateral has moved (change of use does not effect filing).

b) A Copy of the signed Financing Statement must be re-filed in the new county within the 4 Month period in order to continue effectiveness of filing (i.e. perfection).

c) The S/I may be "re-perfected" in the new county after the 4 Month period, in which case, Perfection Date = Time of New Filing (in the new county) (thus, you lose priority to any Lien Creditors who 'attach' in before the new filing).

(*** Note: Change of Use does not impair the effectiveness of the original filing.)

(4) **Filing Requirement:** §9-103 determines whether filing is necessary in the state.

(5) **Transmitting Utilities and Fixture Filing:**

a) The proper place for filing a Fixture or Transmitting Utility is the Secretary of State.

b) This section is Subject to §9-302(3)

c) This section supersedes any previous sections above (i.e. §9-401)

(6) **Residence** - (see also 9-103)

a) For purposes of this section, the Residence of an Organization is

1) It's place of business (if it has only one)

2) Where its Chief Executive Office is (if it has more than one place of business)

b) Use this subsection only if Alternatives II or III of §9-401(1) are used.

§9-402: The Financing Statement:

(1) **Requirements of a Financing Statement:**

a) Required Contents:
1) Signatures, Names and Addresses of Debtors
and 2) Names of Secured Parties
and 3) Address of Secured Pty who can supply information about the S/I (to others)
and 4) Description of Collateral, *either*
a. Describing the items of collateral
or b. Indicating the types of collateral
and 5) Additional details of collateral required:
a. Description of Real Estate - for Crops
b. Must comply with§9-402(5) for
1. Natural Resources (oil, gas, minerals, timber)
2. Accounts subject to §9-103(5)
3. Fixture Financing Statement (as per §9-313) for goods which are (or will become) fixtures

b) A Financing Statement may be filed *before*:
1) A Security Agreement is made
or 2) A S/I otherwise Attaches

c) **Using a Security Agreement as a Financing Statement:**
1) A copy of the Security Agreement can serve as a valid Financing Statement if:
a. It contains the above information (in (1))
and b. It is signed by the Debtor
2) A photocopy or carbon copy of the Security Agreement is also valid (as a Financing Statement) if:
a. The Security Agreement allows
or b. The original had been filed in the state

(2) **Absence of Debtor's Signature:** A Financing Statement (complying with (1) (above)) signed by the Secured Pty but not the Debtor is only sufficient to perfect a S/I in:

(a) Collateral which is/was already subject to a S/I in another jurisdiction when:

1. It is brought into the state

or 2. Debtor's location is changed to that state

(*** Note: Financing Statement must say that the collateral was brought into this state or that the Debtor's location was changed to this state under such circumstances)

or (b) Proceeds under §9-306 if the S/I in the original collateral was perfected.

(*** Note: Financing Statement Must describe original collateral)

or (c) Collateral as to which filing has lapsed (Note: The S/P Must be re-file)

or (d) Collateral acquired after Debtor changed his Name, Identity, or Corporate Structure

(3) Complying Financing Statement Form * * *
(For detail see model format in statute; see also "UCC Form 1" financing statement)

(4) Amending the Financing Statement:

a) F/S may be amended by filing an amendment which is:

1. In Writing

and 2. Signed by both the Debtor and Secured Pty

b) Amendments do not extend the period of the F/S's effectiveness

c) Amendments adding collateral are effective as of the filing date of the amendment (i.e. perfection date for priority purposes is NOT the original perfection date for the new collateral)

d) Whenever "Financing Statement" is referred to (in Article 9), it includes the original F/S and all amendments.

(5) Financing Statements Requiring Real Estate Description:

1) Financing Statements must describe Real Estate for collateral of
   - a) Natural Resources (oil, gas, minerals, timber)
   - b) Accounts subject to §9-103(5)
   - c) Fixture Financing Statement (as per §9-313) for goods which are (or will become) fixtures

2) F/S Requirements:
   - a) Show that it covers this type of collateral
   - and b) Recite that it is filed in the Real Estate records
   - and c) Give enough detail of the Real Property -sufficient to give Constructive Notice of the mortgage or Real Property (pursuant to the state law)

3) If the Debtor does not have an interest of record in the land then F/S must show the name of a "record owner" (of the property)

(6) Fixture Filing Mortgages:

i) A Mortgage is effective as a F/S for Fixture Filings from the date of its recording if:

   - (a) The goods are described in the mortgage by item or type
   - and (b) The goods are to become (or already are) fixtures related to the Real Estate described in the mortgage
   - and (c) The mortgage complies with this section's requirements for a F/S (except that it need not state that it is to be filed in the Real Estate office)
   - and (d) The mortgage is duly recorded

ii) A fee for filing the F/S is not required; only the regular recording and satisfaction fees with respect to the mortgage are required.

(7) **Identity of the Debtor**

a) A F/S will be deemed to sufficiently show the identity of a Debtor if it gives the Individual, Partnership, or Corporate name of the Debtor (whether or not it adds other trade names or partners. Trade name alone is not adequate).

b) If Debtor changes its name, identity, or Corporate Structure (ex: merges) to the point that a filed F/S becomes *seriously misleading* then:

1. Perfection will be lost for all collateral acquired by the Debtor *more than* 4 Months *after* the change, *unless* 2. a new, appropriate F/S is filed within the 4 Months after the debtor changes his name/identity.

c) The F/S need not be change if a Debtor transfers the collateral (even if Secured Pty knows/consents to transfer) (Note: This does not apply to After-Acquired Property. A new F/S must be filed to perfect After-Acquired Property.)

(8) A F/S which contains *minor errors* is still valid if

a) It *substantially* complies with this subsection

and b) Errors are not *seriously misleading*

(must identify Creditor only enough to identify them or be able to contact them)

§9-403: Filing Process:

(1) Filing occurs upon:

a) Presentation of a F/S for filing

and b) *Either:*

1) Tendering the filing fee

or 2) Accepting the F/S by the Filing Officer

(2) Duration of Filing:

a) A filed F/S is effective for 5 Yrs. from the filing date (subject to (6) below).

b) A Continuation Statement must be filed *before expiration* of the term (5 Yrs.) in order to continue perfection (i.e. the F/S's effectiveness)

c) If an Insolvency Proceeding occurs, the F/S will be effective until the *later* of:

1. The expiration of the 5 Yr. filing period

or 2. 60 days after the proceedings have terminated

d) Upon lapse, the S/I becomes Unperfected, *unless* it is perfected without filing (ex: by possession).

e) A S/I which becomes unperfected due to lapse, is deemed to have always been unperfected when dealing with a person who became a Lien Creditor or a Purchaser *before* it lapsed.

(3) **The Continuation Statement**

a) A Continuation Statement (C/S) may be filed by a Secured Pty within 6 Mos. *prior to* the expiration of the 5 Yr. period

b) **Requirements of a Continuation Statement:**

1. Be signed by Secured Pty

and 2. Identify the original F/S by file #

and 3. State that the original statement is still effective

c) A C/S which is signed by a person who is not a Secured Pty must

1. Be accompanied by a written statement of assignment (complying with §9-405(2)), signed by Secured Pty

and 2. Include payment of the required fee

d) Upon filing of the C/S, the Perfection period is extended for another 5 Yrs. (from the date of expiration (not 5 Yrs from filing of the C/S))

e) Subsequent C/S's may be filed (in the same manner) to continue perfection

f) A F/S may be removed or destroyed if

1. It has expired over a year ago

or 2. It is preserved on microfilm (or other photographic record)

(4) Duties of the Filing Officer: (subject to (7) below) A Filing Officer shall:

a. Mark each statement with an assigned file # and time of filing

and b. Retain a copy of it on record or on microfilm *for public inspection*

and c. Index the F/S by Debtor's name (indicating the file # and address of Debtor in index)

(5) Filing Fee * * *

(Note: there is usually a higher fee for filing a non-standard F/S form (i.e. filing the S/A as the F/S))

(6) Exceptions to 5 Yr. Perfection Period:

a) If Debtor is a Transmitting Utility (pursuant to §9-401(5)), the F/S may allow perfection to remain effective until a Termination Statement is filed

b) A Mortgage filed as a Fixture Filing (as per §9-402(6)) is effective until:

1. The mortgage is released or satisfied

or 2. Its effectiveness otherwise terminates as to the real estate

(7) Indexing Records

a) The Filing Officer shall index the F/S in the same manner as mortgages are indexed (as if the Debtor and S/P were a mortgagor and mortgagee respectively) for collateral consisting of:

1) Natural Resources

2) Accounts subject to §9-103(5)

3) Fixture Financing Statement (as per §9-313) for goods to become fixtures

b) If a state requires, the F/S shall be indexed under

1) The Debtor's name (as if he were the mortgagor)

and 2) The Secured Pty's name (as if he were a mortgagee)

§9-404: The Termination Statement:

(1) **Demanding the Termination Statement**

a. **Consumer Goods**:

1. The S/P must **File** a Termination Statement (wherever he filed a F/S) within 1 Month or within 10 Days after S/P receives a Written demand for the Termination Statement if:
    - a) There is no outstanding Secured Obligation
    - and b) There is no commitment to make advances, incur obligations or give value
    - and c) The F/S covers Consumer Goods
    - and d) The original Financing Statement was filed after the effective date of the Revised Article 9
2. Each Termination Statement must:
    - a) State that the Secured Pty no longer claims a S/I under the F/S
    - and b) Include the Filing Number of the original F/S

b. **Other Cases** (Non-Consumer Goods):

1. Within 10 Days of Debtor's Written demand, the S/P must **Send** to the Debtor one Termination Statement for each F/S he filed
2. Each Termination Statement must
    - a) Include the Filing Number of the original F/S
    - and b) State that the Secured Pty no longer claims a S/I under the F/S
3. The S/P must only comply with Debtor's demand if:
    - a) There is no outstanding Secured Obligation
    - b) There is no commitment to make advances, incur obligations or give value

c. **Signature**:

1. The Termination Statement should be signed by the S/P.
2. A Termination Statement signed by another person will be valid only if:
    - a) It is accompanied by a separate <u>written</u> Statement of Assignment, signed by the S/P
    - and b) The Statement of Assignment complies with §9-405(2)
    - and c) Payment of the required fee is included

d. **Penalty For Noncompliance**: If, upon Debtor's demand, the S/P fails to comply with this subsection, the S/P shall be liable for:

1. A $100 penalty
2. and 2. Any loss caused to the Debtor by S/P's failure to comply

(2) <u>Filing The Termination Statement</u>

a. Upon presentation, the Filing Officer must note the Termination Statement on the index.

b. If the officer has received 2 copies of the Termination Statement, he shall return the copy to the S/P, *stamped*, to show when it was received.

c. **Removal of records**

1. The Filing Officer may remove original records from the file at any time after the receipt of the Termination Statement *if* the Filing Officer has a copy (on microfilm or other photographic records) of the:
    - a) Financing Statement
    - and b) Continuation Statement
    - and c) Statement of Assignment
    - and d) Statement of Release

2. If there are No photographic records, the officer must wait at least <u>1 Year</u> after receiving the Termination Statement before removing the originals from the files.

(3) **Filing Fee** * * *

§9-405: Assignment Of Security Interest:

(1) **Assignment on the Financing Statement**

a. An Assignment of a Security Interest may be disclosed by

1. Indicating the *Name* and *Address* of the Assignee on the F/S

or 2. By attaching a copy on the face or the back of the F/S

b. The Filing Officer shall mark the F/S upon presentation (pursuant to §9-403(4))

c. Fee Schedule * * *

(2) **Statement of Assignment**:

a. A S/P may assign - *on the record* - all or part of his rights under a F/S by filing a Separate Written **Statement of Assignment**

b. The Statement of Assignment must

1. Be in Writing

and 2. Be signed by the Secured Pty of Record

and 3. Set forth the Name of the Debtor and Secured Pty of Record

and 4. Include the File # and Date that original F/S was filed

and 5. Contain the Name and Address of the Assignee

and 6. Describe the collateral assigned

c. A Copy of the Assignment may be used if it contains the required information (as stated above).

d. Upon presentation of the Statement of Assignment, the Filing Officer shall:

1. Mark the Statement with the date and hour of filing

2. Note the Statement of Assignment on the Index *either:*

a) Under the Name of the Assignor (as Grantor) - for Assignments of

1) Fixture filings

2) Filing covering timber to be cut

3) Minerals (or the like)

4) Accounts subject to §9-103(5) (filing where Debtor lives)

*** Note: Must also index the Financing Statement under the name of the Assignee if the state requires filing assignments of mortgages under the assignee's name

or b) Under the Financing Statement - for all other filings

3. An Assignment of Record - for a S/I in a Fixture (perfected by including the fixture on a mortgage filing (see §9-402(6)) may only be made by assigning the Mortgage (as provided by the law of the State)

4. Fee Schedule * * *

(3) The Assignee will become the "Secured Pty of Record" after disclosure or filing of an assignment under this section.

§9-406: Release Of Collateral:

1) A S/P of Record may release all or part of any collateral described in a filed F/S by signing a **Statement of Release**

2) The Statement of Release must contain:
   a. A Description of the collateral being released
   and b. The name and address of the Debtor
   and c. The name and address of the Secured Pty of Record
   and d. The file number of the F/S

3) **Signature**
   a. The Statement of Release should be signed by the S/P
   b. A Statement of Release signed by another person will be valid only if:
      1) It is accompanied by a separate written Statement of Assignment, signed by the S/P of record
      and 2) The Statement of Assignment complies with §9-405(2)
      and 3) Payment of the required fee is included

4) **Filing the Release**
   a. Upon presentation of the Statement of Release, the Filing Officer shall:
      1. Mark the Release with the date and time of the filing
      and 2. Note the Release on the Index of the Financing Statement

   b. Fee for Filing the Release * * *

§9-407: Information From Filing Officer: (**)

(1) Upon request, the Filing Officer shall give the person filing the F/S a copy of it, with the filing time and date stamped on it (this rule shall also apply to Statement of Assignment, Termination Statement, and Statement of Release).

(2) Upon request of any person, the Filing Officer shall issue a Certificate showing whether there is any effective F/S naming a particular Debtor, and the time and date on which each F/S was filed.

§9-408: Financing Statements For Consigned Or Leased Goods:

1) A Consignor or Lessor of goods may file a Financing Statement using the terms "consignor," "consignee," "lessor," "lessee" or the like, instead of the terms specified in §9-402 (i.e. "Debtor" and "Secured Pty")

2) Although Part 4 of Article 9 shall apply to such a F/S, the filing of a F/S shall not - of itself - be a factor in determining whether or not the Consignment or Lease is intended as a Security Interest (as per §1-201(37)).

3) If it is eventually determined (for other reasons) that the consignment or lease is actually a Security Interest, the S/I attached to the goods will be *perfected* by the filing of this financing statement.

PART 5:

DEFAULT

§9-501: Rights and Remedies of Parties Upon Default:

(1) **S/P's Right's and Remedies**:

a. When a Debtor is in Default under a S/A, the Secured Pty has rights and remedies provided by this Part.

b. The S/P's rights and remedies may be expanded in the S/A, yet, these rights will be subject to §9-501(3).

c. S/P's Available Remedies

1. Reduce his claim to judgment

or 2. Foreclose

or 3. Enforce the S/I by any available judicial procedure

or 4. If collateral is Documents, he may proceed as to the documents *or* goods covered by them.

d. A S/P in possession of collateral has rights, remedies, and duties as provided by §9-207

e. The remedies listed above are cumulative (i.e. they may be used together)

(2) **Debtor's Rights and Remedies:** Upon default, the Debtor has rights and remedies as provided by:

a. This Part

and b. The S/A

and c. §9-207

(3) **Non-Waivable Rights and Duties**

i) **Rights and Duties Which Cannot be Waived:**

(a) S/P's duty to Account for any Surplus Proceeds of Collateral (§9-502(2) and §9-504(2)).

(b) Rights and Duties concerning Disposition of Collateral (§9-504(3) and §9-505(1)).

(c) Rights and Duties concerning Acceptance of Collateral as Discharge of Obligation (§9-505(2)) ("Strict Foreclosure").

(d) Rights to Redeem Collateral (§9-506).

(e) S/P's liability for failure to comply with these Default rules (as per §9-507(1)).

ii) The rules listed above cannot be waived since they require the S/P to perform special duties and give the Debtor special rights.

iii) **Exceptions** - The above Rights and Duties may be waived or changed when dealing with:

a) *Compulsory Disposition of Collateral* (as per §9-504(3) and §9-505)

or b) *Redemption of Collateral* (as per §9-506)

iv) Standards of Measurement: The parties may determine, by agreement, the *standards* by which these rights and duties are to be measured - as long as those standards are *not manifestly unreasonable*.

(4) If the S/A covers both Real Property and Personal Property, the S/P may *either:*

a) Proceed under the UCC (Article 9, Part 5) only for the Personal Property

or b) Proceed under the State's Real Property law for both Personal and Real Property (in which case, this Part does not apply)

(5) **Judicial Lien or Sale**:

a. When a S/P has reduced his claim to judgment, the Judicial Lien of a Levy made upon his collateral (for his benefit) will *Relate Back* to the date of Perfection of the S/I (in the collateral)

b. Judicial Sale

1. A Judicial Sale is considered to be a "Foreclosure of the S/I by judicial procedure" (within the meaning of this section).
2. The S/P may purchase his collateral at the sale.
3. If the S/P buys the collateral, he may take it free of any other requirements of Article 9.

§9-502: Collection Rights Of Secured Parties:

(1) In the event of Default, or when so agreed, the S/P may:

a. Notify the Account Debtor (or the Obligor on an Instrument) to make payment to him for the outstanding debt (regardless of who was collecting payment for the indebtedness)

or b. Take Control of any Proceeds which he is entitled to (under §9-306)

(2) S/P's Options:

a. The S/P may, *by agreement*:

1. Be entitled to charge back uncollected collateral

or 2. Have full or limited recourse against the Debtor

or 3. Undertake to collect from the Account Debtor or Obligors

b. If the S/P is entitled to any of the above options,

1. He must proceed in a *Commercially Reasonable Manner*

and 2. He may deduct his reasonable expenses of realization from the collections

c. If the S/A secures an indebtedness

1. The S/P must Account (i.e. return) to the Debtor for any Surplus

and 2. The Debtor will be liable for any deficiency (unless otherwise agreed)

d. **Exception:** The Debtor will not be liable for any Deficiency and the S/P will not be obligated to return any Surplus if:

1. If the S/A does not specifically require

and 2. The underlying transaction is *either*

a) Sale of **Accounts**

or b) Sale of **Chattel Paper**

§9-503: Secured Party's Right To Take Possession After Default:

1) The S/P has a right to take possession of collateral upon default (unless otherwise agreed).
2) The S/P may proceed to take possession without judicial action if it can be done *"without breach of the peace."*
3) The Security Agreement may require the Debtor to make the collateral available to the S/P at a designated, mutually convenient place.
4) A S/P may render Equipment unusable or dispose of collateral (as per §9-504) on the debtor's premises if it cannot be removed.

§9-504: Secured Party's Right To Dispose After Default:

(1) Disposition of Collateral:

i) Upon default, a S/P may sell, lease, or otherwise dispose of collateral, *either:*

a. In its present condition

or b. Following any *commercially reasonable Preparation or Processing*

ii) Any sale of goods is subject to the Article on Sales (Article 2)

iii) Proceeds of the disposition shall be applied in the order of the following:

(a) **Selling Expenses** - the reasonable expenses of retaking, holding, preparing for sale/lease, and selling/leasing (including reasonable attorney/legal expenses involved (to the extend provided for by S/A (and not prohibited by law)))

(b) **Satisfaction of Debt** - under his Security Agreement

(c) **Satisfaction of other Debts** - secured by any *Subordinate* S/I holders if:

1) Written notice of demand is received before distribution of the proceeds is completed

and 2) Reasonable proof of S/I is presented (upon S/P's request)

(2) Deficiency and Surplus:

a) If the S/I secures an Indebtedness, then, **unless otherwise agreed**:

1) The Debtor is entitled to surplus of the sale from the S/P

and 2) The S/P (seller) is entitled to deficiency from the Debtor

b) If the underlying transaction was a Sale of Accounts or Chattel Paper then, **ONLY if the Security Agreement provides**:

1) Debtor is entitled to surplus of the sale from the S/P

and 2) S/P (seller) is entitled to deficiency from the Debtor

(3) Notice of Disposition:

a) Disposition may be made by public or private proceedings.

b) Disposition may be made as a one whole sale, or in separate transactions (under separate contracts).

c) Disposition sale must be made under any *commercially reasonable* terms (including the method, manner, time, and place of the sale)

d) S/P is not required to sell all collateral to one party.

e) Secured Pty must notify Debtor of time and place of sale *unless:*

1) Debtor agrees not to be notified after default

or 2) Collateral is perishable

or 3) Collateral is very sensitive to market (value changes quickly)

or 4) Collateral is of a type customarily sold on a recognized market

f) Notification:

1) For *Consumer Goods*, no other notification must be sent

2) For all other goods, notification must be sent to all other Secured Ptys who sent Selling S/P a written notice of claim of an interest in the collateral.

g) The S/P may purchase the collateral:

1) At any **Public Sale**

or 2) At a **Private Sale**, if

a. The collateral is of the type sold in a recognized market

or b. The collateral is of a type which is subject to a widely distributed standard price quotation

(4) Even if the Secured Pty files to make a proper sale, a Purchaser takes Free of the S/P's (and any other subordinate's) right/interest in the collateral if:

(a) Collateral sold public sale:

1) Collateral is sold at a Public Sale.

and 2) Purchaser has no knowledge of any defects in sale process.

and 3) Purchaser does not buy in collusion with another Secured Pty, the person conducting the sale, or other bidders.

and (b) The Purchaser acts in Good Faith (in all other sales (i.e. private sale)).

(5) Non-Qualifying Sales or Dispositions:

a) A Person has rights and duties of a S/P if:

1) She is liable to a S/P under either a:

a. Guaranty

or b. Indorsement

or c. Repurchase Agreement

or d. The like

and 2) She *either:*

a. Receives a transfer of collateral from the S/P

or b. Is subrogated to her rights

b) Such a transfer of collateral is not considered to be a "Sale or Disposition of Collateral" under Article 9.

§9-505: Disposition Of Collateral:

(1) Compulsory Disposition Of Collateral

a) A S/P who has taken possession of the collateral must dispose of it under §9-504 within 90 Days after he takes possession if:

1) The Debtor has paid 60% of *either:*

a. The cash price of a Consumer Goods PMSI

or b. The loan of any other S/I in Consumer Goods

and 2) The Debtor has not signed a statement after default, renouncing or modifying his rights under this Part

b) If the S/P does not dispose of the collateral (pursuant to §9-504) within 90 Days, the Debtor may recover on the S/P's liability either

1) In conversion

or 2) Under §9-507(1)

(2) Acceptance of Collateral as Discharge of Obligation

a) In all other cases (not specified in §9-505(1)) the S/P may propose to retain the collateral as Discharge of debtor's obligation (i.e. Strict Foreclosure)

b) Notice:

1) If the Debtor has not signed a statement renouncing or modifying his rights under this subsection, the S/P shall, after default send written notice of his proposal (to keep the collateral in satisfaction of the debt).

2) **Additional Notice:**

a. Consumer Goods: No other notice is required

b. Other Cases: S/P must send a copy of the notice to all other Secured Parties who:

1. Have sent the S/P a written notice of their claim to interest in the collateral

and 2. S/P has *received* the notice *before either:*

i) The Debtor renounced or modified its rights

or ii) S/P sends Debtor notice to accept collateral as discharge.

3) If anyone entitled to receive notice (including Debtor) objects to the S/P's proposal within 21 Days after notice was *sent*, S/P must dispose of the collateral (under §9-504).

4) The S/P may keep the collateral in satisfaction of the Debtor's obligation if he does not receive any written objection (within 21 days).

§9-506: Debtor's Right To Redeem Collateral:

1) Unless otherwise agreed in writing, after default, the Debtor or any other Secured Pty may redeem the collateral at any time *before*:
   - a) The S/P has disposed of the collateral
   - and b) The S/P has entered into a contract for the collateral's disposition (as per §9-504)
   - and c) The obligation has been discharged (as per §9-505(2))

2) The party redeeming the collateral must pay
   - a) *All* of the obligations secured by the collateral (i.e. debt is "accelerated," and debtor must pay all of his debt, not just the missed installments)
   - and b) Expenses *reasonably incurred* by the Secured Pty while
     - 1) Retaking the collateral
     - and 2) Holding the collateral
     - and 3) Preparing the collateral for disposition
     - and 4) Arranging for the sale
   - and c) Reasonable attorney fees and legal expenses (to the extent provided in the agreement, and not prohibited by law)

§9-507: Secured Party's Liability For Failure To Comply:

(1) If it is established that the S/P is not proceeding in accordance with this Part, then:
   - a. If Disposition has not occurred - it may be ordered or restrained (i.e. by legal action, on appropriate terms and conditions)
   - b. If Disposition has already occurred - the following parties may recover *any loss caused* by S/P's failure to comply with this part:
     - 1. The Debtor
     - or 2. Any party entitled to notification
     - or 3. Any party whose S/I had been made known to the S/P before the disposition
   - c. If collateral is Consumer Goods, the Debtor has a right to recover:
     - 1. An amount not less than: The credit service charge + 10% of the principal amount of the debt
     - or 2. The time price differential + 10% of the cash price

(2) **Commercially Reasonable Manner**

a. The fact that a better price could have been obtained had the S/P chosen a different method or time for the sale, does not - of itself - prove that the sale wasn't made in a Commercially Reasonable Manner.

b. A S/P is deemed to have sold the collateral in a Commercially Reasonable Manner if:

1. The S/P sells the collateral in the usual manner in any recognized market

or 2. He sells it at the current Market Price (at the time of the sale)

or 3. He sells it in conformity with *recognized commercial practices* among Dealers in the type of property sold

or 4. The disposition is approved

a) In any Judicial Proceeding

b) By any Bona-fide Creditor's Committee

c) By any Representative of Creditors

(*** Note: Approval is not required for a disposition to be deemed Commercially Reasonable)

c. The above two rules also apply to other types of disposition when appropriate.

SELECTED BANKRUPTCY STATUTES

§544: Avoiding Powers:

(a) Trustee's Avoidance Powers:

i) At commencement of the case, the trustee shall have the

1. Rights and powers of any Creditor
2. Right to avoid any transfer of debtor's property
3. Right to avoid any obligation incurred by the Debtor

ii) These powers are received regardless of the trustee or any Creditor knowledge

ii) Scope of Voidability: Avoidance powers apply to obligations/transfers that are voidable by:

(1) A Creditor that:

a) Extends credit to Debtor by petition date

and b) Obtains a Judicial Lien with respect to such credit

1. At petition date

and 2. On all property on which a Creditor on a simple contract could have obtained such a judicial lien -- regardless of whether a Creditor actually exists (i.e. a "Hypothetical Lien Creditor")

or (2) A Creditor that:

a) Extends credit to Debtor by petition date

and b) Obtains an execution against the Debtor that is returned unsatisfied -- regardless of its actual existence (i.e. "Hypothetical Lien Creditor")

or (3) A Bona-Fide Purchaser of Real Property (other than fixtures) that buys from a Debtor:

a) Against whom applicable law permits such transfer to be perfected

b) That obtains the status of Bona-Fide Purchaser

c) Who has a perfected such transfer by petition date - regardless of whether or not such a purchaser actually exists (i.e. "Hypothetical Lien Creditor")

(b) The Trustee May Avoid:

1. Any transfer of interest of the Debtor in property

or 2. Any obligation/debt incurred by the Debtor that is

a. Avoidable (under applicable law) by an unsecured Creditor under §502

or b. Not allowable only under §502(e)

<u>§546: Exceptions To Avoiding Powers:</u>

(a) An action (under §544,545,547,548,or 553) must be commenced *after* the <u>earlier</u> of:

(1) <u>2 Yrs.</u> after Trustee's appointment

(2) The time the case is closed or dismissed

(b) <u>Trustee's avoidance powers are subject to:</u>

1) Any generally applicable law permitting perfection to relate-back in time (thereby allowing a later S/I to be effective against an earlier interest in the same property).

2) An interest in property shall be perfected by notice if:

a) Such law dictates that perfection can only be accomplished by *either:*

1. Seizure of property

or 2. Commencement of an action

and b) There has been no seizure or commencement by petition date.

3) Notice must be made within the time fixed by such law requiring seizure or commencement (for perfection).

(c) <u>Reclamation Rights</u>:

The rights and powers of a trustee (under §544(a), 545, 547, and 549) are subject to any rights (Statutory or Common Law) of a <u>*Seller of Goods*</u> to reclaim goods sold to Debtor.

(1) **Requirements:**

a. Goods are sold in the Ordinary Course of Seller's Business

and b. Debtor received goods while insolvent

and c. Seller makes a <u>written</u> demand within <u>10 Days</u> after Debtor receives goods

(2) Seller's Right to Reclamation may be denied if court

(A) Grants seller's claim under §503(b)

or (B) Secures seller's claim by a lien

(d) Crops * * *

(e, f) Trustee Cannot avoid Margin Payments * * *

(g) Trustee Cannot avoid "Swap Agreements" * * *

§547: Preferences:

(a) Definitions (Note: These definitions apply to the bankruptcy provisions.)

(1) **Inventory** - Personal Property which is:
- a. Leased or furnished
- b. Held for sale or lease
- c. To be furnished under a contract for service
- d. Raw Materials
- e. Work-in-process
- f. Materials used or consumed in business
- g. Farm products held for lease (such as crops or livestock)

(2) **New Value:**
- a) This includes:
  - 1) Money
  - 2) Money's worth in goods, services or new credit
  - 3) Release by a transferee of property (which was previously transferred to it in a valid transaction by the Debtor (or trustee under applicable law)) including Proceeds of such property.
- b) An obligation substituted for an existing obligation is not considered New Value.

(3) **Receivable** - a right to payment (whether or not such right has been earned by performance)

(4) A Debt for a tax is incurred on the day when such tax is last payable *without penalty* (including any extensions).

(b) Voidable Preferences: A Trustee may avoid any transfer of interest of the Debtor, in property which is:

(1) To or for the benefit of a Creditor

and (2) For/on account of an *Antecedent Debt* (i.e. past debt owed by Debtor before transfer was made; not a contemporaneous transaction(under §547(c)(1)))

and (3) Made while the Debtor was insolvent (under 547 (f))

and (4) Made *either:*

(A) Within 90 Days of petition date

or (B) Between 90 Days to 1 Year of petition date for "*Insiders*" (as per BRC §101)

and (5) A transfer that enables the Creditor to receive more than he would if:

(A) The case were under Chapter 7 (Liquidation; i.e. the Creditor is not over-secured under §725)

and (B) The transfer had not been made

and (C) Creditor received payment of debt under this title

(c) **Exceptions:** (Savings Clauses)

(1) Contemporaneous Exchanges: Transactions will be considered contemporaneous *to the extent* that they were *both*:

(A) Intended to be a ***Contemporaneous Exchange*** for **New Value** (ex: a check which is cashed within 30 days after it is exchanged is considered contemporaneous)

and (B) In fact a *substantially* contemporaneous exchange (see 547(e))

(2) Ordinary Course of Business: Transfers qualify if:

(A) It was a payment of a Debt that was incurred in the *Ordinary Course of Business*

and (B) It was made in the *Ordinary Course of Business* or financial affairs of the Debtor and the Transferee (ex: regular Bond payments, regular installments on a loan)

and (C) Made according to Ordinary Business Terms

(3) PMSI's: Qualify only if:

(A) The S/I secures *New Value* that was:

(i) Given At or After signing a S/A (S/A must contain description of new collateral)

and (ii) Given by the Secured Pty

and (iii) Given as a PMSI (i.e. to enable Debtor to acquire property)

and (iv) Was actually used by Debtor to acquire property (i.e. a "true PMSI").

and (B) It was Perfected within 20 Days after the Debtor receives possession of the property

(4) New Value: A transfer given to the Creditor who gave *New Value* **after** Debtor made the transfer, if:

(A) The new value was not secured by an *unavoidable* (i.e. not perfected) S/I (and therefore subject to the avoiding powers under §546)

(B) The Debtor did not make the Creditor better off than he would have been if the Creditor did not give the Debtor new value (ex: over secures, to extend to past debts)

(5) Floating Liens: New **Perfected** S/I's in Inventory or Receivables *including their proceeds*: As long as the S/I does not prejudice unsecured creditors by "over-securing" to cover debts made during the LATER of:

(A) *Either:*

(i) 90 Days before the petition date (for a transfer applying to §547(b)(4)(A))

or (ii) 1 Year before the petition date, if the transfer was made by an *"insider"* (as per §547(b)(4)(B))

(B) The date that *New Value* was first given under the S/A to create the S/I

(6) Unavoidable Statutory Liens (pursuant to §545) (ex: statutory liens)

(7) Payments to Ex-Spouse * * *

(8) Property of a Personal Debtor if:

a) Debtor's debts are primarily Consumer Debts

and b) The total value of all affected transferred property is < $600

(d) Avoiding Transfers to a Surety

1) The trustee may avoid a transfer of an interest in the Debtor's property which is to or for the benefit of a Surety if:

a) It is to secure reimbursement of such a Surety

and b) The Surety furnished a bond or other obligation to dissolve a Judicial Lien (which the trustee could have avoided under §547(b)).

2) The liability of the Surety under such a bond/obligation shall be *discharged* to the extent of *either:*

a) The value of such property recovered by the trustee

or b) The amount paid to the trustee

(e) **Time of Transfer** (for purposes of this section)

(1) **Perfection:**

(A) **Real Property** (other than fixtures): Perfection occurs when a *Bona-Fide Purchaser* who buys from the debtor (against whom applicable law permits such a transfer to be perfected) cannot acquire an interest that is superior to that of the Secured Pty (i.e. when the transaction is recorded).

(B) **Personal Property** (including fixtures): Perfection occurs when a Creditor cannot acquire a superior Judicial Lien to that of the Secured Pty (i.e. the S/I is perfected so that it is superior under UCC §9-301(1)(b)).

(2) **When Transfer is Made**:

(A) When transfer is actually made, if its perfected within 10 Days of transfer

or (B) Upon Perfection, if perfected **after** 10 days after transfer

or (C) Immediately before petition is filed If is NOT perfected by the *later* of:

(i) The commencement of the case (petition date)

or (ii) 10 Days after the transfer is actually made

(3) Debtor must acquire rights in property for transfer to be made.

(f) Preference Period: Debtor is presumed to have been insolvent within 90 Days immediately preceding petition date (for purposes of this section)

(g) Burden of Proof: For purposes of this section,

1. The Trustee has the burden of proving avoidability of a transfer under §547(b).
2. The Creditor (or party in interest against whom recovery or avoidance is sought) has the burden of proving non-avoidability under §547(c).

§548: Fraudulent Transfers:

(a) A Trustee may avoid Transfers made within 1 Yr. of petition date if the Debtor:

(1) Made the Transfer with Actual Intent to **Hinder, Delay** or **Defraud** any other Creditors (including those created after transfer)

or (2) *Either:*

(A) Received *less than reasonably equivalent value* (in exchange for the transfer/obligation)

and (B) The Debtor was *either:*

(i) Insolvent *either*

1) As a result of transfer/obligation

or 2) When the transfer was made

or (ii) Undercapitalized

or (iii) Creditor knew or should have known Debtor couldn't "afford" the transfer

(b) Trustee of a Partnership - A Trustee can generally avoid transfers by an insolvent partnership to a General Partner if the debtor was insolvent when the transfer was made (or became insolvent as a result of the transfer).

(c) Exception: Unless a Trustee can avoid the transfer (under §544,545,546, or 547), a creditor may avoid a transfer if it takes the Transfer or Obligation:

1) For New Value
2) In Good Faith
3) For a "fair" price

(d) (1) **Time of Transfer** (for purposes of this section):

a) A Transfer is made when it is so perfected that even a Bona-Fide Purchaser who buys from the Debtor (against whom applicable law permits such a transfer to be perfected) cannot acquire an interest superior to that of the Transferee.

b) If such a transfer is not so perfected (as indicated above) before the petition date, then the transfer will be deemed to have been made immediately before the date of the filing of the petition.

(2) Other Terms * * *

APPENDIX

Special Time Periods

A. **10 Days**

1. Security Agreement's for Consumer Goods can only secure After-Acquired property acquired by Debtor within 10 Days after the S/A is made (§9-108)
2. **Proceeds**: Temporary perfection; If required, you have 10 Days to re-perfect (file/possession) to maintain continuous priority (§9-306(3))
3. **Non-Instrument PMSI** - 10 Days after Db receives *possession* to file/perfect a Non-Instrument PMSI (§9-301(2); §9-312(4)), for priority to date back to attachment
4. **Termination Statement** - must be sent to Debtor within 10 Days after Debtor requests one (§9-405)

B. **21 Days**

1. **Instruments, N/D's:** Temporary Perfection; Must perfect within 21 Days of attachment for priority to date back to attachment (§9-304(4))
2. **Debtor's Possession of Collateral**: If Db takes possession of collateral perfected by possession, you must file if Db take it for more than 21 Days. (§9-304(5))
3. **PMSI in Instruments** - must perfect within 21 Days of possession for super-priority/attachment; must give other Cr's letter before this period (§9-312(3))
4. **Response to Secured Pty's proposal** - A person may respond or object to a Secured Pty's written proposal to keep collateral in exchange for discharging his claim within 21 Days after receiving S/P's proposal.

C. **30 Days**

§9-103(c) - Multi-State PMSI agreements: If collateral does not end up in proposed state within 30 Days after Db take **possession**, Cr must re-file.

D. **45 Days**

Future Advances must be perfected within 45 Days after a lien Creditor or purchaser arises **(§9-301(3); §9-307(3))**

E. **90 Days**

1. **Compulsory Disposition** - A Secured Pty must dispose of collateral (which it has seized upon default) within 90 Days after it takes possession.

2. **Insolvency** - a Debtor is deemed to be insolvent 90 Days before it files its petition Bankruptcy (aka - "Preference Period")

E. **4 Months**

1. Must re-file or make Changes in debtor's name/ID on F/S **(§9-402(7))**
2. **Removal of Collateral** - Must re-file if Debtor moves **(§9-103(1)(d))**

F. **5 yrs.**

Expiration of Financing Statement; must file a **Continuation Statement** *at least* **6 Mos.** before the expiration.

CHECKLIST FOR PERFECTION OF A SECURITY INTEREST

1. Is the Security Interest perfected?
    - a) Attachment:
        - 1) Has a S/A been created (writing/possession)?
        - 2) Has Value been given?
        - 3) Does Debtor have rights in collateral?
    - b) Perfection:
        - 1) Is there a Filing?
        - 2) Is there Possession?
        - 3) Is there Automatic Perfection?
            - a. PMSI Consumer goods
            - b. Proceeds
            - c. After-acquired property
2. Are there any Defenses?
    - a. Does the Creditor own the property ("collateral")?
        - 1. Is it a Lease?
        - 2. Is it a Consignment?
        - 3. Is it a Bailment for service or process?
    - b. Are there any Set-Offs?
3. Are there any exceptions that apply?
    - a. Has the collateral been bought by a Buyer In Ordinary Course?
    - b. Is the debtor in Bankruptcy?

CHECKLIST FOR LAWYER WHEN CREATING A SECURITY INTERESTS

1) Ask about any liens
2) Check records
3) How did seller get the goods?
4) Where will the goods be located?
5) Where will the goods likely be at any particular time?
6) Are there any expiration rules in effect?
7) Do the goods fall into any of the "Special Cases"?

PERFECTION AT A GLANCE

A. **Accounts**: Filing

B. **Chattel Paper**:
1. Filing or Possession
2. Possession is much more preferable

C. **Consumer Goods**: *excluding motor vehicles and fixtures*
1. Automatic Perfection - If a PMSI
2. Filing or Possession - if not a PMSI

D. **Equipment:** Filing or Possession

E. **Farm Products:** Filing or Possession

F. **Fixtures:** Fixture Filing on realty records

G. **General Intangibles:** Filing

H. **Instruments:**
1. Possession only (cannot file)
2. Temporary-Automatic Perfection - for 21 Days after attachment

I. **Inventory:** Filing or Possession of goods

J. **Motor Vehicles:**

1. Compliance with state Certificate of Title laws
2. Filing - if they are inventory of a dealer and have never been issued a Certificate of Title yet

K. **Negotiable Documents:**

1. Possession only (cannot file)
2. Temporary-Automatic Perfection - for 21 Days after attachment

L. **Proceeds:**

1. Automatic Perfection - if goods can be perfected in the same manner and can also be classified under the same description as the original collateral
2. Temporary- Automatic Perfection - for 10 Days in all other cases

Effects of Changes

1. Removal of Collateral §9-103(3) (4 Months)
2. Change of Name - §9-401(3) (4 Months)
3. Change of Form (Proceeds) - §9-306 (10 Days)
4. Transfer of Collateral - §9-401(7) (chg. of state?)
5. Change in use - §9-401(3) (change in filing location?)
6. Transformed to CP

INDEX